Activity Assemblies to Promote Peace

It is imperative and relevant to teach today's children about peace and peaceful strategies, learning to handle conflict creatively, and tackling injustice and racial prejudice. Packed with topical ideas for the primary school teacher, this book offers material for over 40 primary assemblies, easy to use in an assembly or for preparation.

A great resource to dip into for one-off assemblies or follow as a programme of themed assemblies for a term, it is helpfully split into topic areas on peace which include:

- co-operation
- children's writing
- places and challenges
- assembly plays
- environment
- stories.

Each assembly starts with a drama, story or interactive activity, followed by a prayer or 'reflection' and a hymn or a song. There are suggestions for questions and ideas for developing the theme which include making masks and puppets, as well as stories from six major world religions: Christianity, Buddhism, Hinduism, Islam, Judaism and Sikhism.

The book will be invaluable to headteachers, deputy headteachers, primary school teachers or any trainee teacher who is looking for a collection of assembly ideas that promote peace, tolerance and understanding in the widest possible context and in a variety of different ways.

Elizabeth Peirce has extensive teaching experience and was formerly General Primary Schools' Adviser (Early Years) for East Sussex County Council Education Authority. She has written extensively on School Assemblies for the BBC Schools' Radio programmes, magazine articles, and the United Nations Candlelight Vigil Teachers' Pack. Her other books include *Activity Assemblies for Christian Collective Worship 5–11*, *Activity Assemblies for Multi-racial Schools 5–11* and *Multi-faith Activity Assemblies*.

Other books by Elizabeth Peirce

Activity Assemblies for Christian Collective Worship 5–11 (Falmer Press, 1991)
Activity Assemblies for Multi-racial Schools 5–11 (Falmer Press, 1992)
Assembly File, 1 (Folens Limited, 1996)
Multi-faith Activity Assemblies: 90+ Ideas for Primary Schools (RoutledgeFalmer, 2003)

Activity Assemblies to Promote Peace

40+ ideas for multi-faith assemblies
for 5–11 years

Elizabeth Peirce

Routledge
Taylor & Francis Group

LONDON AND NEW YORK

First published 2008
by Routledge
2 Park Square, Milton Park, Abingdon, Oxon OX14 4RN

Simultaneously published in the USA and Canada
by Routledge
270 Madison Ave, New York, NY 10016

Routledge is an imprint of the Taylor & Francis Group, an informa business

© 2008 Elizabeth Peirce

Typeset in Sabon, Garamond and Gill Sans by
RefineCatch Limited, Bungay, Suffolk
Illustrations by Gary Holmes
Printed and bound in Great Britain by
TJ International Ltd, Padstow, Cornwall

British Library Cataloguing in Publication Data
A catalogue record for this book is available from the British Library

Library of Congress Cataloging-in-Publication Data
Peirce, Elizabeth, 1946–
Activity assemblies to promote peace : 50 ideas for multi-faith assemblies
for 5–11 years / Elizabeth Peirce.
  p. cm.
1. Peace–Religious aspects–Study and teaching (Elementary)–Activity
programs. 2. Religions–Study and teaching (Elementary)–Activity
programs. I. Title.
BL65.P4P45 2008
372.84–dc22
                                                         2007048544

ISBN10: 0–415–46682–2 (pbk)
ISBN10: 0–203–92662–5 (ebk)

ISBN13: 978–0–415–46682–0 (pbk)
ISBN13: 978–0–203–92662–8 (ebk)

Contents

High Flight

Oh! I have slipped the surly bonds of Earth
And danced the skies on laughter-silvered wings;
Sunward I've climbed, and joined the tumbling mirth
Of sun-split clouds – and done a hundred things
You have not dreamed of – wheeled and soared and swung
High in the sunlit silence. Hov'ring there,
I've chased the shouting wind along, and flung
My eager craft through footless halls of air . . .
Up, up the long, delirious burning blue
I've topped the wind-swept heights with easy grace,
Where never lark, nor even eagle flew –
And, while with silent, lifting mind I've trod
The high untrespassed sanctity of space
Put out my hand and touched the face of God.

John Magee* in *The Complete Works of John Magee, The Pilot Poet*,
published by This England Books, Gloucestershire, 1989.
Used with kind permission.

* John Magee was a Spitfire pilot who was killed at the age of nineteen during the Second World War.

Introduction

Why peace assemblies?

Teaching about peace and peaceful strategies, handling conflict creatively, recognising one's own strengths and weaknesses, learning to love and forgive others, tackling injustice and demonstrating the futility of violence, seem to be utterly imperative and relevant for children in today's war-torn world.

Daily news bulletins inform us of the lack of peace: man's inhumanity to man; cruelty to children; starving millions; corruption; exploitation; needless, endless wars causing suffering around the world; cruelty to animals; the extinction of rare species of animals and birds; the pollution of our planet; nuclear dumping, etc. How can we begin to change things? There must be a better way. What strategies do we need? How should we begin to teach our children to act and think differently?

My research has led me to look at war and peace from a historical perspective; to look at peace literature; peace poetry; individual contributions from people of peace; peace organisations; how different cultures and religions regard peace. (See also E. Peirce, *Multi-faith Activity Assemblies*, RoutledgeFalmer, 2003.) One thing is clear for us as teachers, there is no place in Society for racism or bigotry. We have to understand one another, our neighbour, our neighbour's religion and that skin colour makes no difference in our peaceful quest. We have to learn a proper respect for all human beings and their points of view. We have to learn to listen and to celebrate our differences and similarities and humanity.

Children need to learn peaceful strategies for themselves. They also need to learn the concept that 'peace starts with me' and 'how I view the world'. In their learning quest, children need to love themselves before they can love others and they need to learn how to put others first, how to be a servant. Not the ingratiating, cringing kind, but the honest, caring individual, truly desiring to make the world a better place in which to live, through their direct actions.

Once the children have understood this concept of peace lying within themselves, they can reach out and spread peace within their families, their homes, their schools and communities and in all their relationships. Finally, attention can be turned to peace in the environment, looking at ecological and global issues. Children need to question what is acceptable and what is not. They need to grow into the sort of people who stand against injustice of any kind. For example, is it right that a chemical factory in Bhopal should wipe out half the population of an Indian village in terrible agonising deaths? Or is it acceptable that children should suffer in Sudan, Iraq, Lebanon, Gaza and all the war-torn areas across the world? Children need to question apartheid, ethnic cleansing, the disappearance of political prisoners and prisoners of conscience; they should be aware of Governments who, today, turn a blind eye to animal cruelty and then tomorrow turn a blind eye to human cruelty.

One person's voice does make a difference. If the world could genuinely, honestly follow the words of Christ, 'Love your enemies, do good to those who hate you, do not repay evil for evil, turn the other cheek', wars could be wiped out altogether. The trouble is, we all fail in this ideal, yet this failure should not prevent us from attempting to do better, to create a better place in which to live, to build a better world. We need to study techniques for dealing with anger, disappointment, grief. We need to learn the value of compromise, communication in the face of injustice, empathy with our fellow human beings and that ultimately we are all responsible for activity or inactivity in our world's dilemmas. So these are my reasons *why* we should teach about peace, now *how* do we go about it?

How do we go about teaching peace through assemblies?

In this book, I have used a variety of methods and techniques for introducing the topic of peace into school assemblies. For example, I have used the 'sermon-type' method, that is where a point to be covered is best articulated by *one person*, perhaps using a traditional overhead projector with pictures, such as in the assembly entitled 'The Tree-Huggers' or those assemblies that make use of a DVD, CD-Rom or a PowerPoint presentation. Or where artefacts are used, such as the sword, shield, helmet, coat of mail, etc. in the assembly entitled 'Paul's Armour'.

Secondly, I have involved *two or three* children to demonstrate an idea, such as the need for co-operation in the story entitled 'The Two Mules'; and a *number of children* to demonstrate a concept such as the lack of peace, in the assembly entitled 'The Dragon at the Wedding'.

Sometimes, I have felt it is appropriate to include the *whole class* in an assembly, such as the one entitled 'Sharing a Meal' on pages 30–33. Or even involve the *whole school* such as in the assembly entitled 'Two Co-Operative Games for a New Term'. 'Rainbow Babies' can also involve the *whole school* as different classes act out the different parts.

Techniques too, have varied. For instance, I have used mime on pages 110–14 where children are encouraged to mime the story of the 'Parable of the Talents', or Dorothy Brooke's pioneering work with cavalry horses in the 1930s.

Drama such as 'The Bishop's Candlesticks' or 'Toxic Waste' has been used to good effect, as has the children's own written work or artwork, in the pieces entitled 'What Peace/ War Means to Me' and 'Writing Peace Poems'.

Fiction and non-fiction can be a rich source of assembly inspiration. The use of picture books in assemblies can be found on pages 151–53, whilst true stories about some of the great lives of people of peace can be found in Part 4.

Poetry too, has been included in a number of the assemblies. These can be used on their own, or as an addition to each assembly. Particularly noteworthy are the Buddhist Meditation (page 43), the Celtic Benediction, 'New Responsibility' by Kate Compston (page 134) and 'Dance in Front of Tanks' by John Emery on page 45.

Puppets, marionettes, masks, shadow puppets and hand puppets can all be used to demonstrate the theme of peace. For example, see 'The Prodigal Son' on pages 13–14 to see how a large hand puppet was used. Further reference to marionettes and shadow puppets can be found in Elizabeth Peirce, *Activity Assemblies for Christian*

Collective Worship and *Activity Assemblies for Multi-racial Schools*, published by Falmer Press, 1991 and 1992.

Posters, Filmstrips, Videos, DVDs, CD-Roms, slide-tape and PowerPoint presentations have all been employed in this collection of assemblies. There are so many useful posters to stimulate discussion or drama in assemblies, for example from Pauline Books and Media, Christian Aid, Cafod, Oxfam, The Quaker Peace and Education Service, art from the National Gallery, and posters of pop stars, great musicians, travel, etc.

Videos such as 'Luke Street' from Scripture Union and slide-tape presentations from Corrymeela have all proved useful. Specific music from the Corrymeela Community, the Iona Community, the Taize Community as well as hymns, modern, popular songs and folk music can all be used in peace assemblies. Music from Jewish, Russian and Irish traditions has also been included or mentioned in the book. The Internet, of course, is an endless source of information and appropriate web-sites have been included wherever possible.

I started this whole collection of ideas with just one word: 'Peace', and an exciting world of interest unfurled!

Peace Topic Web: A Brief Overview

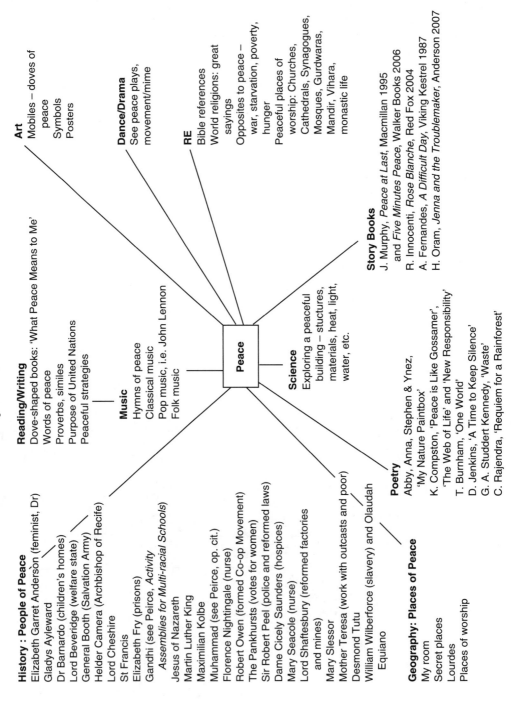

Art
Mobiles – doves of peace
Symbols
Posters

Dance/Drama
See peace plays, movement/mime

RE
Bible references
World religions: great sayings
Opposites to peace – war, starvation, poverty, hunger
Peaceful places of worship: Churches, Cathedrals, Synagogues, Mosques, Gurdwaras, Mandir, Vihara, monastic life

Reading/Writing
Dove-shaped books: 'What Peace Means to Me'
Words of peace
Proverbs, similes
Purpose of United Nations
Peaceful strategies

Music
Hymns of peace
Classical music
Pop music, i.e. John Lennon
Folk music

Story Books
J. Murphy, *Peace at Last*, Macmillan 1995 and *Five Minutes Peace*, Walker Books 2006
R. Innocenti, *Rose Blanche*, Red Fox 2004
A. Fernandes, *A Difficult Day*, Viking Kestrel 1987
H. Oram, *Jenna and the Troublemaker*, Anderson 2007

Science
Exploring a peaceful building – stuctures, materials, heat, light, water, etc.

Peace

Poetry
Abby, Anna, Stephen & Ynez, 'My Nature Paintbox'
K. Compston, 'Peace is Like Gossamer', 'The Web of Life' and 'New Responsibility'
T. Burnham, 'One World'
D. Jenkins, 'A Time to Keep Silence'
G. A. Studdert Kennedy, 'Waste'
C. Rajendra, 'Requiem for a Rainforest'

History : People of Peace
Elizabeth Garret Anderson (feminist, Dr)
Gladys Ayleward
Dr Barnardo (children's homes)
Lord Beveridge (welfare state)
General Booth (Salvation Army)
Helder Camara (Archbishop of Recife)
Lord Cheshire
St Francis
Elizabeth Fry (prisons)
Gandhi (see Peirce, *Activity Assemblies for Multi-racial Schools*)
Jesus of Nazareth
Martin Luther King
Maximilian Kolbe
Muhammad (see Peirce, op. cit.)
Florence Nightingale (nurse)
Robert Owen (formed Co-op Movement)
The Pankhursts (votes for women)
Sir Robert Peel (police and reformed laws)
Dame Cicely Saunders (hospices)
Mary Seacole (nurse)
Lord Shaftesbury (reformed factories and mines)
Mary Slessor
Mother Teresa (work with outcasts and poor)
Desmond Tutu
William Wilberforce (slavery) and Olaudah Equiano

Geography: Places of Peace
My room
Secret places
Lourdes
Places of worship

Part I

Peace Starts With Me

5–7 Years Assembly

Learning to Love Myself

An important peace strategy starts with learning to love oneself. Children need to learn self-esteem before they can love others.

You will need the following costumes

> Butterfly wings
> Robin mask
> Fish tail
> Elephant trunk and ears
> Leotards and tail for kangaroo
> Eight octopus legs
> Tubular worm costume
> Bear mask

You will need the following paper / card

> Large sheets of paper for painting
> Cardboard face cut-outs and pieces of paper to write about 'Five Things I Like About Myself'.

Start the assembly with the hymn *If I Were a Butterfly*.

If I Were a Butterfly

(Brian Howard)

1. If I were a butterfly
   I'd thank you, Lord, for giving me wings.
   And if I were a robin in a tree,
   I'd thank you, Lord, that I could sing
   And if I were a fish in the sea,
   I'd wiggle my tail and I'd giggle with glee,
   But I just thank you, Father, for making me 'me'.

Refrain

   For you gave me a heart
   And you gave me a smile
   You gave me Jesus
   And you made me your child.
   And I just thank you, Father, for making me 'me'.

2. If I were an elephant
   I'd thank you, Lord, by raising my trunk.
   And if I were a kangaroo,
   You know I'd hop right up to you.
   And if I were an octopus,
   I'd thank you, Lord, for my fine looks,
   But I just thank you, Father, for making me 'me'.

Refrain

3. If I were a wiggily worm,
   I'd thank you, Lord, that I could squirm.
   And if I were a fuzzy-wuzzy bear,
   I'd thank you, Lord, for my fuzzy-wuzzy hair.
   And if I were a crocodile,
   I'd thank you, Lord, for my big smile,
   But I just thank you, Father, for making me 'me'.

Refrain

Dress nine children up in the costumes and as each verse is sung, the children could mime the actions of the characters in the song, i.e. a butterfly, a robin, a fish, an elephant, a kangaroo, an octopus, a worm, a bear and a crocodile. (*The whole class could do the actions, if it is decided that everyone could be involved in dressing up.*)

A further nine children could paint pictures of the characters to hold up and to show to the assembled children.

The rest of the children could be encouraged to write about what they particularly like about themselves to read in the assembly.

Questions to consider

What makes each person different or special?
If you could be someone else, who would you be and why?
What do you particularly like about yourself?
What characteristics do you admire in other people?
Think of five things about yourself that are special.

1 --
2 --
3 --
4 --
5 --

Five Things that I Like About Me

End the assembly with simple impromptu prayers from the assembled children, thanking God for something that they particularly like about themselves, e.g. for being healthy, good at football, caring, generous, etc.

Make a Class Book about 'Myself', include personal qualities as well as physical descriptions.

Story

Meek, A., *I'm Special, I'm Me*, Little Tiger Press, 2006.

Winner of the 'Search for a Story' New Author Prize. Tells the story of a Mum giving positive reinforcement to her son in all his changing games at school, until he finally decides that being himself, he can do all sorts of things. Suitable for 5–7 year olds.

Learning to Love Others
Rainbow Babies

This assembly is adapted from a story by Dr Hugh Morgan-Hill in *Spinning Tales, Weaving Hope* published by New Society Publishers, 1992.

This is a drama that could involve the whole class or even the whole school, with each class taking the part of one of the groups suggested below. The action could be performed in the round with each group getting up in turn to perform their mime. Or the action could be performed in the traditional way, at the front, each group entering and miming their part, as the Narrator reaches their particular point in the story. If the drama is to be performed at Christmas, the baby Jesus could be substituted for the Rainbow baby.

You will need the following characters

Group of different nationalities fighting
Group of children playing games
Group of clowns playing tricks / laughing
Group of children singing songs
Group of pets i.e. ponies, rabbits, dogs, cats, white mice, etc.
Black woman
Poor woman
Group of Rainbow babies with pink, green, blue, black, red, brown, yellow painted faces and costumes. (Could also draw or cut-out some paper Rainbow babies.)
Narrator

The story can be mimed as the Narrator tells it.

(Enter group of different Nationalities, who begin fighting.)

Narrator

Once upon a time, a very long time ago, in a country not very far from here, everyone started fighting each other. Neighbours who had been quite good friends began to fight one another for no good reason at all. Some fought each other because they had different coloured skins, some fought each other because they had different religions, some fought each other because they did not like people from other countries. Oh, it was all so awful and there was so much killing and so much sadness and many people died. Then a very strange thing began to happen. Quite suddenly, one by one, all the babies began to disappear. *(Part of the fighting group leaves the stage.)* Then all the children disappeared. *(Another group leaves.)* And very soon there were no young people left at all, only a group of very old people who had done all the fighting. The old people were so shocked by this, that they stopped fighting each other and they began to ask where had their children gone? Who had taken them? (*The action is mimed.*) But nobody knew. Some people said they had been taken away to a different star or planet for safety, until the fighting stopped. Others said it was God punishing them, for being so wicked for fighting in the first place. The people began to wring their hands (*mime action*) and ask each other what they should do. They decided to hold a meeting.

(*The group remaining on the stage now sit down in a circle.*)

Narrator

Perhaps we could get our children back by doing all the things that children love to do, instead of fighting, they decided. So first of all, they decided to play all the children's games. (*The group gets ready to mime what the Narrator says.*) They played hopscotch, bats and balls, skipping, throwing and catching bean-bags, making sand-castles, etc.

(*The group on the stage mime all these different games. The list could be extended to include board games such as chess, draughts, snakes and ladders, tiddly-winks, etc. Then they go and sit down as the Narrator continues with the story.*)

But all these lovely activities failed to make the children return. So the old people sat down again and scratched their heads and thought what else could they do? (*The action is mimed.*) 'I know', said one old person, 'children love laughter, if we do funny things and tell jokes and laugh a lot, perhaps the children will come back then?'

(*Enter a group of clowns who do handstands and cart-wheels and forward rolls, who hold their tummies and imitate laughter.*)

But even this funny spectacle failed to make the children return. So the old people sat down once again and scratched their heads and wondered what they could do? (*The action is mimed.*) 'I know', said one old person, 'if we all sing the children's favourite songs that will surely make them return, they won't be able to resist joining in.'

(*The group of children who are to sing, enter and stand in the middle of the stage; or stand up if the drama is in the round. They sing some of the old favourites with the appropriate actions e.g.:*

In and out the dusky bluebells
The farmer is in his den
There was a lovely princess
Ring-a ring-a roses
Old Macdonald had a farm
Ten green bottles
The Grand old Duke of York, etc.)

Narrator

But even all this lovely singing failed to make the children return. So the old people said, 'What on earth can we do now that we haven't tried already? Can we try one more thing to make our children come back?' The old people thought and thought again.

'I know', said one old person, 'children love animals and pets. Let's gather as many animals as we can and fill our land with lovely creatures, surely this will make our children return.' So the people brought cats and dogs, rabbits and horses, white mice and budgerigars, hamsters and guinea-pigs, tortoises and monkeys, etc.

(As the Narrator names the pets, children wearing different costumes, masks, face-paints etc. process round the hall in a colourful pageant, or toys could be used.)

Narrator

But still the children and babies did not return. Then, from out of nowhere, there came the most beautiful black lady, whose eyes shone like stars and who was expecting a baby. All the old people came to look at her, they were terribly excited, perhaps God had forgiven them and they would start having children born in their land again.

The people all brought expensive presents to the Mother-to-be and laid them at her feet. The presents became more and more expensive and extravagant, until someone brought a silver tricycle covered in diamonds (*a bike covered in foil could be used*), everyone gasped, but when they looked at the beautiful black lady, they saw that she was crying. Huge tears were trickling down her lovely face. What was the matter? She didn't speak, she just kept crying. Then, from out of the crowd, came a very poor, ragged-looking woman, who also didn't say a word, but, by her movements and the look in her eyes, you could see she was filled with love for the black lady. She lovingly put her arm around the black lady's shoulders and she gave her some bread to eat and some warm milk to drink.

You see the black lady didn't want the expensive gifts, she just wanted to be shown love and she wanted to know that if her baby was born in that country, the baby would be loved by everyone and that the fighting would end.

Suddenly everyone understood, it was love, not war that their own children needed. This is what would bring them home.

The beautiful black lady had her baby and do you know it was a rainbow coloured baby (*or Son of God, if this option is chosen*). Yes, really, the baby was red and orange and yellow and green and blue and indigo and violet. And the people loved him. They cuddled him and gurgled at him and tickled his tummy (*The baby is held high and shown to the audience*).

The black lady smiled when she saw that the people loved her rainbow baby. She also knew that they really loved her, so she made them promise not to fight anymore about colour of skin, or race or religion and then they would have babies of their own. All the people in the land promised to do this and quite suddenly, out of the sky, came hundreds of babies with red and black and orange and brown and blue and green faces. Some babies were even rainbow coloured.

(The drama ends with the entrance of all these children with different coloured faces, dancing around the stage and hugging each other.)

Reflection

End with a time of quiet to consider the serious message of not fighting someone because they are different from us, or use the prayer or poem below.

Prayer

Father God, forgive us when we fight and quarrel especially over the colour of some-one's skin, or country of origin, or particular religion. Forgive us Father and help us to live in harmony with our neighbours. For world peace begins with me and how I treat my brothers and sisters, friends and neighbours. Bless each one of our homes and bring us your peace and harmony. Amen

Hymn

No. 538, 'Peace I Give To You' in *Mission Praise*, published by Marshall Pickering.

Poetry

Read the poem below, 'Let Peace Fill Our Heart', part of a longer poem entitled 'Lead Me From Death To Life' by Liz Birtles in *Voices Speaking Peace* compiled by E. Birtles, published by The Unitarian Peace Fellowship, 1990. Reproduced with kind permission of the author.

Let Peace Fill Our Heart

Let peace fill our heart
our world our universe.
Peace begins with me.
I must start with my own heart and mind.
I need to practise the skills necessary for living in a world at peace,
the skills needed to avoid or resolve conflicts.
The place to begin my work is in my own home,
in my personal relationships, in my place of work,
in my church.
Peace begins with me
and works outward,
nurtured by the pervading power of the loving Spirit
which connects all people.
Lead me O God.

Jealousy

One of the emotions that consistently destroys a sense of personal peace is feelings of jealousy. Children have to learn coping strategies to deal with this common emotion. One way is to confront their feelings openly and plainly and thereby deal with negative thoughts (*see list one below*) and turn them into positive thoughts (*see list two below*). Harbouring feelings of jealousy inevitably leads to disharmony and ultimately to quarrels, so must be dealt with, if peace is to be achieved.

For this assembly, let the children make their own two lists (*the teacher could make two large posters or use OHP sheets for the two lists, for demonstration purposes*). One list is entitled a 'Green-eyed Monster of Jealousy', a list of things that make them feel jealous. The second list, a 'Multi-petalled Daisy', is a list of blessings that they possess, to combat any negative thoughts. For this second list, encourage the children to think of blessings not only as their material possessions, but also their own abilities; their senses like sight, taste, touch, smell, hearing; their friendships; their qualities, etc. (A daisy is a useful mnemonic because it is a common flower and many-petalled.)

Finally, children who feel they are unloved, can be reminded that God's love is always consistent, by reading the following extracts from the bible:

Isaiah Chapter 43 verses 1–4. The prophet Isaiah reminded the people of Israel that whatever happened, God would always love them. 'These are the words of the Lord, your creator, the one who made you', he said. 'Fear not, for I have redeemed you; I have called you by name, you are mine. When you pass through the waters I will be with you; and through the rivers, they shall not overwhelm you. . . . For I am the Lord your God . . . you are precious in my eyes and honoured, and I love you.' (RSV)

Jeremiah Chapter 31 verse 3. Another prophet, Jeremiah, proclaimed that God said 'I have loved you with an everlasting love'. (RSV)

Choose two or three children who have made their lists, to read them to the assembled children and end with the poem 'Grudges' by Judith Nicholls.

Grudges

It isn't fair . . .
that I must be in bed
for hours before,
that I get all the blame
and never her,
that she's allowed to choose
what she will wear,
it isn't fair!

It isn't right . . .
that she's allowed out
late at night,
that she can *choose* when to
switch off her light,
that I'm the one told off
whenever there's a fight,
it isn't right!

It makes me mad . . .
that they think she's so good
and I'm so bad,
that she gets extra cash
for helping dad,
that *her* old coats are all
I've ever had,
it makes me mad!

(I know I'm nine
and she is seventeen;
that's no excuse at all
for them to be so MEAN!)

© Judith Nicholls 1994 from *Storm's Eye, published by Oxford University Press.*
Reprinted by permission of the author.

Prayer

Father God, help us to remember whenever we feel jealous, lonely, unloved, or sad, that you will always love us and that you want us to remember that your love is always consistent, never-changing and all-embracing. Thank you. Amen

Hymn

No. 61, 'Glad That I Live Am I' in *Morning Has Broken*, Schofield and Sims Ltd.

Further development

A useful addition to this assembly can be made by reading the story *Pig Tale* by Helen Oxenbury published by Heinemann 2004. It is a lovely story about two pigs who thought the grass was greener on the other side of their gate. They were jealous of those who had riches, fast cars and fancy clothes until they realised just how happy they were right back where they had started, in their own muddy field.

Other stories in the Bible about jealousy could include Joseph and his brothers, Cain and Abel, etc. Or stories about friendship like Jonathan and David could be researched.

Sometimes I am a jealous green-eyed monster. I am jealous of my brother, when my friend does better than me, when someone has nicer clothes, or toys, or sweets. When my teacher says well done to someone else.

List One: Green-eyed Monster of Jealousy

List Two: Multi-petalled Daisy List of Blessings

Forgiveness
The Prodigal Son

Life-size puppets (Muppet-like in character), can be obtained from a number of sources. (See address lists below, for current prices.) This story was dramatised using the 'boy' puppet as the 'really wild' prodigal son for both Infants and Juniors.

This is a story to show that however naughty we have been, if we ask God, our Father, for His forgiveness, he will always forgive us and go on loving us. Jesus told this story. It can be found in Luke Chapter 15, verses 11–32.

A man had two sons, the older boy always worked hard on the farm. The younger boy was a bit of a wild thing. He said, 'Dad, give me my share of my inheritance money now, I don't want to have to wait until I'm older.'

So the father divided his money and gave the youngest son his half. The young son left home and set off for a far country. He spent all his money on wild living.

He bought new clothes, a baseball cap, sunglasses, drinks (*show cans of drink*), computer games, CDs, DVDs, etc. (*Show a variety of expensive items. It is a good idea to ask the children at this point, what they would buy if they had lots of money.*) He bought gifts for all his friends, but soon they all left him.

Then one day, he realised he had no money left (*turns out pockets*). He had to search for work, so that he could make enough money to buy food. He found a job with a pig farmer. It was dirty and smelly work, nobody spoke to him or fed him. He could not buy any food because there was a famine in that land. He would have gladly eaten the pods that the pigs were eating. He was tired and hungry and dirty and smelly and lonely.

Suddenly he had a bright idea. He knew that his father's workmen were given good food to eat and were paid well. He thought that he would go back home, say that he was very sorry to his Dad and ask him if he could just work, like one of his Dad's servants. He would not expect to be treated like his father's son again, or live in his father's house.

So he set off for home. While he was still a long way off from his father's house, his father saw him coming and he ran to meet him. His father threw his arms around his wasteful son and he hugged and kissed him.

The boy said, 'Father, I am sorry, I have sinned against you and against Heaven. I am not worthy to be called your son. Can I work for you like one of your hired servants?' His loving father completely forgave his son and called the servants to bring his son the best robe and put it on him, to put a ring on his finger and sandals on his feet and even gave a special feast to celebrate his son's homecoming and he told them, 'For this is my son who was dead and is alive again, he was lost and now he is found'. (RSV)

The author gave her puppet a name, like Luke, to help the children to remember where the story can be found in the Bible. It also helped the children to identify with a 'real' character who was a rather naughty boy.

Reflection

The assembly could end with a time of quiet to consider God's goodness in forgiving us when we do wrong and how we could do better in the future. Think about those people to whom you might have caused pain and unhappiness. How could you make amends?

Or you could end with the prayer below.

Prayer

Loving Heavenly Father, thank you so much, that when we say we are sorry, you forgive us again and again and run out to meet us and shower us with good gifts. We can have peace with you and with ourselves, knowing that we are forgiven when we go wrong. Help us to forgive others when they go wrong, just as you have shown us to do. Amen

Hymn

No. 410, 'I'm Forgiven' in *Mission Praise*, published by Marshall Pickering.

Addresses for puppets

Puppets By Post
PO Box 106
Welwyn Garden City
Hertfordshire AL6 0ZS
Tel: 01438 714009
Fax: 01438 717484
e-mail: info@puppetsbypost.com
web-site: www.puppetsbypost.com

MITCH Puppet Ministries
16 New Street
Dudley
West Midlands DY1 1LP
Tel: 01384 234408
e-mail: mitchpuppets@lineone.net

Bonds Puppets
(Trades from Jubilee Market, Covent Garden and will post puppets to UK only)
Tel: 07939 493683
e-mail: larry@bonds.wanadoo.co.uk
web-site: www.bondspuppets.com

Time to Sow
PO Box 216
Stotfold SG5 4WZ
Tel/Fax: 01462 639829
web-site: www.timetosow.com

Coping with Disappointments

One of the hardest things a child has to learn is that the world is not fair. In this section of 'Peace Starts With Me', children have to learn coping strategies when things go wrong, or do not work out the way that they should, or the way that they want them to work out.

Tell the following true story.

The Raffle Ticket

It was an extremely exciting day. There were about three thousand children and parents in the auditorium of this magnificent city theatre. Lights sparkled and twinkled all around the domed ceiling, like stars in the heavens; eager faces were now leaning forward over balcony balustrades. The atmosphere was hot with all the laughter of the just-finished performance and a hush had descended upon the entire audience as they waited with eager anticipation for the final duty of the Master of Ceremonies.

It had been a wonderful show and now the moment had arrived for which all the children, at least, had been waiting. The Master of Ceremonies was about to draw the winning raffle ticket for the smartest bicycle you had ever seen.

Everyone held their breath, the ticket barrel was turned over and over on its hinges, so that all the raffle tickets were jumbled together, then the trap door was carefully opened, the Master of Ceremonies gave a final stir to the folded tickets inside and then he held one ticket aloft between the forefinger and thumb of his right hand. He held his hand up high, so that all the watching eyes could see, then very carefully and slowly, he brought his hand down and with his left hand, he opened up the ticket. 'White ticket number 393', he shouted in a very loud voice. 'I've got it', whispered a little girl called Mary in the back row of the second tier balcony. She sat very still for a moment, too stunned to move and then she cried, 'Oh please let me through' as she tried to scramble over legs and bags and coats and people. The Master of Ceremonies was already inviting the lucky winner to join him on the stage to collect her prize.

Mary was still struggling to reach the upper auditorium door at the back of the theatre. There was a lot of clapping in the well of the theatre far below her. 'They must be clapping for me', she thought as she managed to reach the stairs and began to jump down them, two or three at a time. She burst through the lower auditorium door and raced up the centre aisle to the steps leading onto the stage, which the clowns had used earlier in the performance.

And then she stopped, frozen with horror: there on the stage was another little girl and the Master of Ceremonies had already given her the bike. The other little girl was trying to ride the bike around the stage and was wobbling to the laughter and claps of the audience. 'But I have the winning ticket', Mary cried faintly to the Master of Ceremonies. 'Now go away little girl', he said in a not unkind, but rather irritated fashion. 'Can't you see that this little girl has the winning ticket, number 393?'

The children and parents in the auditorium were now getting out of their seats and beginning to make their way along the aisles to the Exit signs, before catching buses and trains to go home. The other little girl on the stage was being led away by her Mum, pushing her treasured prize.

Mary began to cry, she rushed forward to the Master of Ceremonies and showed him her ticket. 'You said, white ticket number 393, I have got white ticket number 393, there must be two tickets with the same number on them.'

'Impossible', said the Master of Ceremonies, who had now decided that Mary had gone quite far enough and was becoming a nuisance. 'Please look at my ticket', she pleaded through her tears, 'I know I'm not wrong.' The lady and her daughter were disappearing off the stage, the Master of Ceremonies began to wish them a safe journey home, whilst reluctantly looking at Mary's ticket. The bright lights in the theatre had all been turned on now to help the audience find their way out and to leave the theatre safely. The bright lights also showed, without a shadow of a doubt, that Mary was holding the winning ticket.

'My goodness, she's right you know, call that other little girl back at once.'

Looking very annoyed, the mother and the other little girl were brought back onto the stage by one of the stage-hands, who had managed to stop them leaving the theatre. 'Let me see your ticket', the Master of Ceremonies commanded. The other little girl felt in both her coat pockets and eventually the ticket was found in the top pocket of her blouse and was produced. 'Number 393' the other pair said triumphantly, but Mary said quietly, 'But yours is pale green, mine is the winning white ticket.' At once the Master of Ceremonies realized that in the dim lights of the auditorium, the ticket had looked white and not pale green and he had made a mistake.

The other little girl began to howl and scream, 'You can't take my bike away, you gave it to me, everyone saw you give it to me – send that horrid little girl away. It's not my fault. It's all your fault.'

The Master of Ceremonies hesitated for a minute and then he said to Mary, 'Look I'm very sorry – but we have given the prize to this other child – we will make it up to you somehow. You can't have this bike now and unfortunately we can't get you another one as we just haven't got the funds – but we will think of something and send it to you through the post.'

Mary was still crying, but reluctantly she agreed to let the other child keep the bicycle and she gave the Master of Ceremonies her home address. A few days later, a large brown paper parcel arrived in the post. Mary ripped off the paper with eager anticipation. It was a large box of face paints. Ordinarily, Mary would have loved a box of real theatrical face paints, but it wasn't the bike that she had set her heart upon.

Can you imagine Mary's disappointment?
How would you have coped with such bad luck?
What would you have done?

The Teacher needs to help the children think through and face some of these issues. Of course there are no easy answers, but somehow, children must be helped to cope with their disappointments by positive thinking if they are to have any peace.

Trying to stand in the other person's shoes can sometimes be a starting point, i.e. just think that you were the other little girl in the story, who was given the prize and then someone came along to try and take it away from you, after it had actually been given to you – how would you feel?

Was anyone to blame or was it a genuine mistake? Could the mistake have been prevented? What about the final gift? What positive attitudes/actions could flow through this gift? (i.e. fun and games with many friends etc.)

There is always someone worse off than oneself – what about all those children who didn't win anything at all?

The assembly could be closed by reading the humorous/disappointed poem entitled 'The Hippopotamus's Birthday'.

The Hippopotamus's Birthday

He has opened all his parcels
  but the largest and the last,
His hopes are at their highest
  and his heart is beating fast.
Oh happy Hippopotamus
  what lovely gift is here?
He cuts the string. The world stands still.
  A pair of boots appear.

Oh little Hippopotamus
  the sorrows of the small.
He dropped two tears to mingle
  with the flowing Senegal –
And the 'Thank you' that he uttered
  was the saddest ever heard
In the Senegambian jungle
  from the mouth of beast or bird.

E. V. Rieu from 'The Hippopotamus's Birthday' and Other Poems about Animals and Birds compiled by L. M. Jennings, published by Hodder and Stoughton Ltd., 1987.

A True Jewish Story from Auschwitz

If one is tempted to ask should we remember Auschwitz, sixty years after the war, or even, is this a suitable story to be told to children, the answer is an unequivocal 'yes'. The lessons learned here should be taught to successive generations to prevent such horrors from ever happening again.

The author visited the 'death' camp and discovered that even in this grisly place, love and light still overcame evil. One kind act will be remembered for all eternity. The first story is told here, the second appears later on in the book on page 64.

Before the assembly, it is necessary to do some background reading and research. There are some excellent web sites to help you in the resources section, which are packed with information. The briefest background details are given here before telling the story.

Auschwitz was a 'death' camp where Nazis exterminated over one million people, mainly Jews from all over Europe. Also Soviets, Czechs, Yugoslavs, Turks, Greeks, Gypsies, French, Austrians, Germans, Poles, etc. were sent there. Perhaps a large map could be pinned up and ribbons stretched from the country of origin to Auschwitz in Poland.

The prisoners were transported in railroad trucks on a 'death' route that led right into the concentration camp of Auschwitz 11 or Birkenau for 'selection'. Those men, boys and some women and girls who were capable of hard physical labour, were ordered to stand on one side of the platform, the remaining men, women, children, elderly and sick were ordered to go and stand on the other side.

Approximately 75 per cent of each train delivery of people were sent immediately to their deaths. Even before the able-bodied marched off to the camps, the chimneys were already excreting the thick black smoke of the burned bodies of their dearly beloved wives, husbands, children, elderly parents or disabled friends. Up to 10,000 people were gassed each day in the 'shower rooms'.

Life in the camp, for those who survived, was appalling. Heads were shaved and each prisoner was issued with filthy rags not fit for the poorest beggar, in exchange for their own clothes. Food consisted of watery soup and a small piece of bread once a day. Everyone had to work on all kinds of exhausting physical tasks imaginable. The guards were evil and cruel, often selecting criminals to rule over each hut to meter out further punishments. Punishments were so despicable. Some people were shot, or tortured or disfigured or maimed or beaten or slowly starved to death.

Surprising then, that down the years, the story of one little boy's love and generosity has survived and is remembered by those who now act as guides round the camp. A child's most treasured possessions in this dreadful place were his bread and his shoes. With these two items, he could survive a little longer. Bread gave him life; his shoes protected his feet from the bitterest, coldest conditions, enabling him to walk and defy the 'death' selection. Visiting in January in temperatures of minus 6, the author had some idea of the extreme bitterness of the snow, wind and ice that seemed to burn any exposed area like the face. But these children had nothing and certainly no warm clothes for protection.

So it was then, that when this little boy received his life-sustaining, meagre piece of bread, his only ration for the whole day and night, that would just about keep him alive, he noticed opposite him a poor, scraggy little girl who had missed out on the rations and she had nothing at all to eat. She stared at him with longing, pleading eyes to be given the tiniest scrap of bread.

The little boy, realising that she would die if she did not eat, broke off a tiny piece of his own and gave it to her. Just at that exact moment, one of the guards witnessed what he had done. He beat the boy unmercifully and as a punishment, he made him stand outside all night in the bitter cold without his shoes, in temperatures of minus 15. As a result, his feet were so badly frost-bitten that he never walked again.

We know this story is true, because we saw a short black and white film of the boy being examined by a Doctor at the end of the war.

But that little boy's one act of kindness and generosity will be remembered by countless millions who now visit Auschwitz and of course by you and me.

The light of human kindness still shines out of the darkness of evil.

Song

Sing 'Zog Nit Keynmol' (words and music below). Or it can be found in *The World's Most Popular Jewish Songs*, Tara, 1997. Angela Wood says that this song is often sung on 'Yom Hashoah' (Holocaust Day) – 'it is an affirmation of the survival of life and hope'. The lyric is in Yiddsh, and here is a pronunication guide:

a	'a' as in 'fah'	l'fahed	'l' 'fah', guttural 'h'; 'ed' as in 'head'
az	'az' pronounced 'as'	letstn	as in 'lets' plus 'n'
blayene	'blay' ryhmes with 'day'; plus 'un'	lo	as in 'low'
		m'od	'muh' plus 'odd'
bloye	'bloye' rhymes with 'boy' plus the 'l' and ends with 'a'	mir	rhymes with 'rear'
		nit	as it sounds phonetically
dem	'dem' as it sounds	noch	rhymes with sock
do	'do' as in 'low'	olam	'o' as in 'toe'; 'lam' as it sounds
du	'du' as in 'too'	oysgebenkte	'oys' as in 'toys'; 'g' as in 'guh'; 'ben' plus 'k'
farshteln	'farsh' rhymes with 'marsh', 'tell' plus 'n'	poyk	as in 'oick' plus 'p'
gesher	'gesh' rhymes with 'mesh'; 'er' as in 'bet'	s'vet	as it sounds
		sho	'sho' rhymes with 'show'
geyst	'gey' as in 'gay' plus 'st'	teg	rhymes with 'vague'
ha	'ha' as in 'fah'	ton	'ton' as in 'on' plus 't'
himlen	as it sounds phonetically	trot	as it is written
hotysh	as in 'hottish'	tzar	pronounced 'tz' plus 'are'
keynmol	'keyn' as in 'cane'; mol rhymes with 'doll'	undzer	as it sounds phonetically
		v'haiker	'v'; 'hai' as in 'high' 'ick' as in 'sick' 'er' as 'car'
klal	as it sounds but with long 'aagh' sound	veg	rhymes with 'vague'
kol	'kol' like 'collar'	vet	as it sounds phonetically
kulo	sounds like 'queue' plus 'low'	zenen	as it sounds phonetically
kumen	sounds like 'come in'	zog	rhymes with 'log'

Zog Nit Keynmol

Zog nit keynmol az du geyst dem letstn
   veg,
hotysh himlen blayene farshteln bloye
   teg,
Kumen vet noch undzer oysgebenkte sho,
S'vet a poyk ton undzer trot – mir zenen do!

We must never lose our courage in the fight,
Though skies of lead turn days of sunshine
   into night.
Because the hour for which we've yearned
   will yet arrive,
and our marching steps will thunder: we
   survive!

From land of palm trees to the land of
   distant snow,
We have come with our deep sorrow and
   our woe.
And everywhere our blood was innocently
   shed,
Our fighting spirits will again avenge our
   dead.

The golden rays of morning sun will dry our
   tears,
dispelling bitter agony of yesteryears.
But if the sun and dawn with us will be
   delayed –
Then let this song ring out the call to you
   instead.

Not lead, but blood inscribed this song
   which we now sing,
It's not a carolling of birds upon the wing,
But a people midst the crashing fires of hell,
Sang this song and fought courageous till it
   fell!

So we must never lose our courage in the
   fight,
Though skies of lead turn days of sunshine
   into night.
Because the hour for which we've yearned
   will yet arrive,
and our marching steps will thunder: we
   survive!

Hirsch Glick

Books

Lehman-Wilzig, T. *Keeping the Promise, A Torah's Journey*, Kar-Ben Publishing, Minneapolis, 2003.

This is a wonderful book, with excellent illustrations that could be read in an assembly, on its own merit. It tells the true story of a tiny Torah Scroll belonging to a Rabbi who was taken to Bergen-Belsen Concentration Camp. Eventually, it is given to a young boy in the camp as he studies for his Bar Mitzvah, whilst he is incarcerated. Later, the boy escapes and many years later, he becomes a Professor of Science. He gives the same tiny scroll to Israel's first Astronaut, Ilan Ramon, who takes it with him into space. The saddest postscript at the back of the book records that the spacecraft exploded on re-entering the earth's atmosphere and the scroll is never recovered. However, whilst Ilan Ramon was in the spacecraft, he held up the tiny scroll for all the world to see and told its amazing history.

Schroeder, P.W. and Schroeder-Hildebrand, D. *Six Million Paperclips, The Making of a Children's Holocaust Memorial*, Kar-Ben Publishing, Minneapolis, 2004.

This is another excellent book recording the response of children from a Middle School in Tennessee, to the Holocaust. They could not imagine what six million people looked like, so they decided to collect paperclips to represent every person who was murdered. What they did not expect, was that this would turn into a Memorial that would involve thousands of children and Heads of State across the world. Eventually eleven million paperclips (to represent six million Jews and five million other victims) were collected and are sealed in a geniune German railcar in their school playground. It was a railcar that had actually been used to transport people to the death camps. But in 2001 it made an amazing journey from Germany to the school, to become a permanent Memorial to all those who died in the Holocaust.

Late in 2006, the story was made into a film for general release. It soon won many awards; most notably, Best Film, Best Director, Best Score, Best Documentary Feature at the Rome International Film Festival.

Web-sites

Holocaust Educational Trust. Touring exhibition and resources for teachers.
web-site: www.thinkequal.com
e-mail: info@HET.org.uk

Anne Frank and the Holocaust provides teachers' resources with curriculum links.
web-site: www.annefrank.eril.net

Beth Shalom Holocaust Centre in Nottingham offers school visits for top juniors.
web-site: www.bethshalom.com and www.holocausthistory.net
e-mail: office@bethshalom.com

Holocaust Educational Trust offers teaching aids, a Holocaust Memorial Day Education Pack and produces an excellent book, in conjunction with the NUT, entitled *Paul's Journey* for Year 6 pupils. Based on Paul Oppenheimer's own memories as a Holocaust survivor.
web-site: www.het.org.uk
e-mail: info@HET.org.uk

Imperial War Museum has a Holocaust Exhibition and Education Pack. Survivor visits can be arranged.
web-site: www.iwm.org.uk
e-mail: ir-edu@iwm.org.uk

Simon Wiesenthal Centre – Museum of Tolerance, USA Archive and Resource Centre.
web-site: www.wiesenthal.com
e-mail: library@wiesenthal.net

US Holocaust Memorial Museum offers a free guide for teachers.
web-site: www.ushmm.org
e-mail: education@ushmm.org

Yad Vashem, Israel. Museum, Resource and Education Centre,
web-site: www.yadvashem.org.il

Poems

End the assembly by reading the following poems:

I Believe

I believe in the light,
even when the sun doesn't shine.
I believe in Love,
even when it isn't given.
I believe in God,
even when his voice is silent.

(Believed to be the words written by a child and found in a bombed out air-raid shelter in Germany after the Second World War).

After a While

After a while you learn the difference
between holding a hand and chaining a soul.
You learn love isn't leaning, but lending support.
You begin to accept your defeats
with the grace of an adult, not the grief of a child.
You decide to build your roads on today,
for tomorrow's ground is too uncertain.
You help someone plant a garden
instead of waiting for someone to bring you flowers.
You learn that God has given you the strength to endure
And that you really do have worth.

Author unknown

Part 2

Peace Through Co-operation

The Tale of the Turnip
A Russian Folk Tale

This story of co-operation lends itself beautifully to dramatisation. It can be performed *by* any age group of children, *for* any age group, because the message remains the same; helping one another ultimately leads to success. Visiting Russia recently, we saw a group of adults perform the story for another group of adults and children, with great success and humour.

You will need the following characters

A turnip: child covered in a white sheet with green leaves tied around the top.
Russian Grandfather: Cossack-style dress with boots, hat and waistcoat.
Russian Grandmother: in Russian style, with headscarf, voluminous skirt and apron.
Granddaughter / or son: in similar style, but brighter colours.
Cat: with whiskers, ears and tail, dressed in black leotard and tights.
Mouse: brown leotard and tights, 'Mickey Mouse' ears, tail, and face-paints.
Narrator

Narrator
We are going to tell you a story about how a little help and co-operation from everyone leads to a happy ending. When you hear me say the words, 'they pulled and they pulled', you can all join in with the words and the actions. (*Have a practice run at this point, with all the assembled children repeating the words and making a pulling movement with their hands clasped in front of them.*)

Narrator
Once upon a time, a long way away, in Russia, a Grandfather had been working on his co-operative farm with his family and friends. He had planted many turnip seeds (*enter Grandfather who mimes the action*), he had watered them, weeded them, hoed them and tended them,

carefully. Now it was time to dig the turnips up and send them all to the city market. He saved the very last turnip for his family and friends as he was going to make lots of lovely turnip soup.

(*Grandfather comes to the end of the row, where the child in turnip costume stands firm.*)

Narrator

Grandfather put his fork under the turnip, but it would not budge an inch. He tried loosening the soil all around the vegetable, but still he could not lift the turnip out of the ground. Next he tried pulling the turnip and he pulled so hard that he fell over backwards, but still the turnip remained firmly where it was.

(*Now invite some audience participation.*)

Audience

'He pulled and he pulled, but he couldn't pull the turnip out.'

Narrator

So he called to his wife, the little old Grandmother, to come and help him. (*Enter Grandmother.*) He told her to fix her arms tightly around his waist, to stop him from falling over and to help him pull the turnip out of the ground.

(*Audience participation.*)

Audience

'They pulled and they pulled, but still they couldn't pull the turnip out.'

Narrator

In fact they pulled so hard that both Grandfather and Grandmother fell over, but still the turnip remained firmly in the ground. So the little old Grandmother called to her grand-daughter to come and help. (*Enter granddaughter.*) The little old Grandmother told her granddaughter to fix her arms tightly around her waist, whilst she held on tightly to her husband to prevent them all from falling over. And they . . .

(*Audience participation.*)

Audience

'They pulled and they pulled, but they couldn't pull the turnip out.'

Narrator

In fact they pulled so hard that they *all* fell over, but still the turnip remained firmly in the ground. So the granddaughter called to her friend the little cat to come and help. (Enter cat.) The granddaughter told the cat to fix her arms tightly around her waist, whilst she held on tightly to her Grandmother and her Grandmother held on tightly to her Grandfather and her Grandfather held on tightly to the turnip, to prevent them all from falling over and in order to pull the turnip out of the ground. And they . . .

(*Audience participation.*)

Audience

'They pulled and they pulled, but they couldn't pull the turnip out.'

Narrator

In fact they pulled so hard that they *all* fell over, but still the turnip remained firmly in the ground. So finally, Grandfather scratched his head and said it was just too bad, they couldn't have turnip soup after all and Grandmother said she would go and turn off the water on the stove, which she was boiling for the soup and granddaughter began to cry, because she was terribly hungry and she had been looking forward to having turnip soup, when suddenly the little cat said she had the tiniest friend, a teeny-weeny mouse, who might just make all the difference, if he lent his hands too. So Grandfather reluctantly agreed to try just once more. So the little cat called to her friend the teeny-weeny mouse and told him to hold on tightly to her waist, whilst she held on tightly to the granddaughter and the granddaughter held on tightly to the Grandmother and the Grandmother held on tightly to the Grandfather and the Grandfather held on tightly to the turnip and TOGETHER . . .

(*Audience participation*) 'They pulled and they pulled . . .'

Narrator

. . . and this time the turnip came right out of the ground with a large plopping sound and all the friends fell on top of one another. Grandfather was able to make his famous turnip soup. There was so much soup that not only did all the family have plenty, but also, there was enough soup for all their friends and their neighbours and everyone was joyful and happy.

You see, when everyone lends a hand and helps one another out, there is usually a happy ending.

Reflection

A candle could be lit and a time of quiet could be kept, in order to consider the idea of everyone co-operating with each other and being helpful to one another. Or use the prayer below.

Prayer

Heavenly father, make us ready to help one another, whenever help is needed, so that we can all enter into each other's joy and happiness.

Hymn

No. 98, 'You Shall Go Out With Joy And Be Led Forth With Peace' in *Come and Praise 2*, published by the BBC.

Two Co-operative Games for a New Term

The purpose of this assembly is two-fold. First (floor space permitting), the assembly is intended to help children to participate actively, rather than to sit passively and listen. Second, it is intended to reinforce affirmative and co-operative values. The ideas presented here can be found in Mildred Masheder's excellent book, *Let's Play Together*, published by Green Print, 1989. (Used with kind permission. She has written many other books, namely *Let's Co-operate*, *Freedom From Bullying*, *Let's Enjoy Nature*, etc.)

As this is an activity assembly and potentially, a fairly noisy affair, it is important that the teacher should have a pre-arranged signal for everyone to go and sit down in silence. (This could be practised before the assembly, e.g. 'Stand up, move about, when I shake the tambourine, return to your place immediately, in silence'.)

The first activity is called 'Getting to Know You'. It is suggested that the children walk round the room and shake hands with as many other children as possible, looking into each other's eyes as they do so, giving and requesting each other's names. Then they go and sit down. This is an especially useful game at the start of a new term or a new year.

A second game is called 'Affirmative Names'. This would be a particularly good game to boost the confidence of shy, rejected children. Mildred Masheder suggests that this game is played in small groups where 'each child, in turn, introduces herself by giving one or two affirmative adjectives beginning with the same letter as her first name: for example, Jolly, Jovial Jane, or Handsome, Helpful Harry. In small circles, players can go round remembering each person's name and descriptions. The last one has the hardest task, but the group should help out.' This game could be played more easily in the classroom. However, for this part of the assembly, perhaps the teacher could adapt the idea, by choosing several children to come out to the front and ask the rest of the assembled children to think of kind adjectives to describe each chosen child or group of children. (This would be a good phonic exercise too!)

At the end of the assembly, it is important for the teacher to draw all the threads together, by emphasising the point that whilst it is important that we think of lovely adjectives to describe each other, it is never acceptable to call children by nasty, hateful names and this will not be tolerated in the school community. It is also important to remember the first part of the assembly, that we shook hands with as many people as possible in the assembly hall to show that everyone is welcomed and valued within the school and should be greeted as a friend who is respected and loved. Leave a time for quiet reflection.

The Two Mules

Act out the story of the two mules on the 'Friends' poster (see picture below, reproduced with the kind permission of the Library of the Religious Society of Friends).

You will need the following characters

Two mules
One farmer
Two children to unroll the long message
Narrator

You will need the following props

Two mule masks, brown jumpers, brown tights and long tails
Two bundles of hay
A stick
A short piece of rope
The long message written on a roll of paper with the words:

'CO-OPERATION IS BETTER THAN CONFLICT'.

Narrator

We are going to show you that co-operation, that is helping one another, is better than conflict, that is fighting one another.

Once upon a time, there was a farmer who had two mules. *(Enter farmer with stick, gently prodding two mules to walk in front of him.)*

Farmer

Come along you two, that's enough work for today. I am just going to rope you two together so that you don't run away and then I'm going to give each of you a nice bundle of hay to eat for your supper. Here you are Fred, this is your bundle. *(Farmer places one bundle of hay on the far left of the stage.)*

Here you are Ned, this is your bundle. *(Farmer places the other bundle of hay on the far right of the stage.)*

Now I am going off to have my supper. Enjoy your food, don't fight over each other's hay. Goodnight you two. *(Exit farmer.)*

Narrator

The two mules licked their lips, they loved fresh hay. *(The mules mime the action. They could say 'yum, yum' and rub their tummies!).*

Then they each turned round to eat their own bundle of hay. But the rope was too short and they were jerked back together, unable to reach the hay. They strained a bit harder, but still they couldn't reach their food. *(The action is mimed).*

As you know, mules bray and kick when they get angry, and Fred and Ned were very angry indeed. First Fred let out a long bray and then Ned let out a long bray and then Fred kicked Ned hard with his back legs. Then Ned kicked Fred hard with *his* back legs. They both fell down in a heap and scratched their heads. What could they do? They both had a nice meal waiting for them, but they could not reach it because of the short rope.

(Invite a little audience participation at this point. What do you think they should do? Be prepared for a child to say, 'cut the rope with a knife' or 'take the rope off' etc. Try and elicit the correct answer of helping each other and then carry on with the story.)

Yes, the two mules put their heads together and thought and thought about what they could do. Suddenly, they had the answer. They got up quietly and walked first to Fred's hay and then to Ned's hay. *(The two mules mime the action).*

By helping each other, they both had a very good meal. Now we have got two children who are going to unroll a long message for us all to learn. You can read the words as they appear:

'CO-OPERATION IS BETTER THAN CONFLICT'

Read it again, with everyone saying the words together and give an explanation about what it means. Pin the message up in a prominent position. Ask the children what it says at different intervals throughout the week. If you have the poster of the two mules, pin that up too.

Prayer

Father God, so often when we are selfish and only think of ourselves, things go badly wrong. Help us to work out our problems together, whenever we can. We know from the story today, that we are all better off, when we learn to co-operate rather than fight.

Reflection

Think about ways in which you could co-operate with someone else today. Make a list in your head.

Hymn

No. 37, 'Working Together' in *Every Colour Under the Sun*, Ward Lock Educational.

Development

Ask the children to think of team games where co-operation is better than conflict or play some of the co-operative games suggested by Mildred Masheder in *Let's Play Together* published by Green Print.

Address for poster

The Religious Society of Friends
Friends House
173 Euston Road
London NW1 2BJ
Tel: 02076 631000 Fax: 02076 631001
web-site: www.quaker.org.uk
e-mail: info@quaker.org.uk

Sharing a Meal
The Feeding of the Five Thousand

A drama to involve the whole class and participation by the whole school. The story can be found in all four gospels of the Bible:

Mathew	Chapter 14, verses 13–21
Mark	Chapter 6, verses 32–44
Luke	Chapter 9, verses 10–17
John	Chapter 6, verses 1–13

The point of this story is to develop an attitude of sharing whatever we have with others. And whatever we share, we believe, God can use and bless.

> Give and it will be given to you; good measure, pressed down, shaken together, running over, will be put into your lap.
>
> (Luke Chapter 6, verse 38. RSV)

You will need the following characters

Jesus
12 Disciples
Boy with 5 loaves and 2 fish
5000 people (Depending on the number of children in class to be involved, 6 groups of 5 children could represent the 'companies' who make up the total number of 5000. It can be explained that a company was a group of 50–100 people. The people mime the action and sit down.)
Narrator (If very young children are to perform the play, the Narrator can speak all the parts, whilst the main characters can mime the actions. Older children can act the parts.)

You will need the following props

5 real loaves of bread to share
2 fish made out of clay or paper

Jesus
(*Calls to his Disciples*) Come on, we have had a very long and tiring day, let us go away to a quiet place by ourselves to rest. We can sail across the lake, to a lonely, quiet place that I know.

(The action is mimed, Jesus and the Disciples get into a boat and mime rowing across the water.)

Narrator

But the crowd saw Jesus and his friends leaving and so they ran ahead on foot to the place that they could see that Jesus was making for, so that they could hear him speak again and some of them were hoping that Jesus would heal them.

(The group of people stand up, wave and call out 'Jesus', 'Jesus', 'Help me', 'Teach me', 'Heal me', etc.)

Narrator

When Jesus went ashore, he saw the great crowd of people before him and he felt very sorry for them, because they looked rather like sheep without a shepherd. So Jesus told them to sit down and he began to teach them many things.

(The crowd sits down, Jesus mimes the teaching.)

Three Disciples

(In unison) Jesus, Jesus, it is getting very late, send all these people away now, to their own homes and villages. They must have something to eat.

Jesus

Well, if they need food, you give them some.

4th / 5th Disciple

How can we? Shall we go to the village and buy £200 worth of bread to feed them?

Jesus

Go and see how many loaves the people have brought with them.

Narrator

The Disciples went up and down the rows of people asking them if they had any bread.

(The action is mimed by the disciples, the people shake their heads in turn. Until one little boy, carrying a small basket, produces 5 loaves and 2 fish. The 6th Disciple takes the boy back to Jesus.)

6th Disciple

Jesus, this young boy has brought 5 loaves and 2 fish and he says that we can all share them.

7th Disciple

(Laughing) But this food won't go anywhere amongst this huge crowd of people.

Narrator

Jesus beckoned the boy to come to him. He took the basket of bread and fish and, breaking the bread into pieces, he thanked God and asked him to bless the food. Then he commanded the people to sit down in companies.

Jesus
(*Holding the food*) Heavenly Father, we thank you for this food and we ask you to bless it, for our use. Amen.

Narrator
Then Jesus gave the Disciples some bread and fish to give to all the seated people.

(If real bread is used, a small piece of bread can be broken off and distributed by each 'Disciple' to all the children in the play and then to the whole assembled school. This can be a very effective way of involving everyone, although the teacher needs to stress that Jesus performed a real miracle by giving so many people something to eat, and that the teacher had bought enough for all the assembled children.)

Narrator
Everyone ate the food and they were fully satisfied and do you know that the Disciples had to gather up twelve baskets of scraps of fish and bread after everyone had *finished* eating!

Teacher
God loves us when we are generous with what we have. We can all share with those who have nothing.

(Perhaps a modern day 'miracle' could be described, such as the generous giving by small children of 'shoe-boxes' filled with good things for the children in war-torn areas. Or perhaps the teacher could use this occasion to ask for support for such a project.)

Prayer

Jesus, help us to be generous with what we have and to share all things with those that have nothing. Amen.

Hymn

No. 457, 'Jesus Put This Song Into Our Hearts' (Graham Kendrick, Thank You Music, 1986) in *Mission Praise 2* published by Marshall Pickering; or No. 139, 'Now the Harvest is All Gathered' in *Come and Praise 2*, published by the BBC (see over).

Now the Harvest is all Gathered

1. Now the har - vest is all ga - thered,   Let us eat the Shar - ing Bread,   In our fam - 'ly all to - ge - ther,   As our cus - tom is, we said.   And we pass the Bread a - mong us,   Thank - ing God that all are fed. ___

1. Now the harvest is all gathered,
   Let us eat the Sharing Bread,
   'In our family, all together,
   As our custom is,' we said.
   And we pass the Bread among us,
   Thanking God that all are fed.

2. But there comes a gentle knocking,
   Just before we break the Bread,
   From our neighbours in the doorway:
   'Harvest failed for us,' they said.
   So we share the Bread among them,
   Thanking God that all are fed.

3. Soon we hear a growing murmur,
   As we eat the Sharing Bread,
   From the neighbours of our
      neighbours:
   'We are starving, friends,' it said.
   Then we stretch the Bread out further
   Thanking God that all are fed.

4. When the world begins to clamour,
   We cry, 'Take our Sharing Bread,
   Miracles we cannot offer!'
   'Oh, it happened once,' they said,
   'Thousands of us ate together
   Thanking God that all are fed.'

Words: © Arthur Scholey;
Music: Douglas Coombes © Lindsay Music (Members of CCLI).

Conquering Fear Together

The purpose of this assembly is to show the children that together they can become strong and overcome whatever frightens them. (Based on an idea by Doug Lipman.)

You will need

  A wicked old woman
  A kind, fairy godmother
  A large group of children who hold hands, sing and do the actions
  Narrator

Narrator
Once upon a time, a group of children were frightened about going to school because they had to pass by the house of a wicked old woman, whom they had heard would eat up children for dinner.

  (*Enter group of children, each running past the old woman's house, shouting something like 'I'm scared, I don't want to go past that old lady's house', 'Help, help', 'Don't eat me up', 'I'm frightened', etc.*)

Narrator
Until one day, one brave child said, 'This is no good, we can't go on like this, we must get some help. Let us go and see my kind fairy godmother, who lives down the road.' (*The action is mimed and the group of children knock on the godmother's door.*)

First child
Please can you help us, we are frightened of that old woman down the street. We don't like going past her door to go to school. What can we do?

Fairy godmother
I know how to help you. But you must do exactly what I say. The only way that you can conquer your fear and make her disappear, is to all hold hands and help each other. She does not like children who help each other. Next, there are three magic things that you must do to make her get smaller and smaller. I will tell you the first magic thing, but you must find out the two other things for yourselves. Do you know the song 'Here we go round the Mulberry Bush'? (*Children nod, perhaps the assembled children could sing one verse.*) Well, whilst you are still holding hands, you must sing the words 'Oh we can hop on one leg, one leg, one leg, Oh we can hop on one leg, on a cold and frosty morning' and you must do the actions at the same time. Shall we have a practice? (*Children sing and practise.*)

Narrator

So the children, still holding hands, went on their way to school, past the wicked old woman's house, when suddenly . . . .

Wicked old woman

Aha, come here you horrible lot. I'm going to eat you all up for my supper. Come on, who is going to be first? Let me catch one of you.

Group of children

(*Still holding hands, hop and sing*) Oh we can hop on one leg . . . . .

Wicked old woman

Oh what is happening to me, I seem to be getting smaller? Oooh, er, help! You may be able to hop on one leg, but I bet you can't jump whilst you are still holding hands?

Group of children

(*Holding hands, jump together and sing*) Oh we can jump up and down, up and down, up and down, Oh we can jump up and down on a cold and frosty morning!

Wicked old woman

What? What? Oh, er, I seem to be getting even smaller, what is happening to me? Oooh, er, help! Well, you may be able to jump, but you certainly won't be able to skip together, so I will finally eat you all up in one big mouthful.

Group of children

(*Holding hands, skip together and sing*) Oh we can skip together, skip together, skip together, Oh we can skip together on a cold and frosty morning.

(*As the children skip, the old woman disappears leaving her hat and cloak centre stage.*)

Narrator

The old woman had completely disappeared and the children were never frightened ever again. But if anything else should happen to frighten them, they knew exactly what they had to do. They would hold hands and sing together.

Prayer

Sometimes, Father God, we get frightened by silly things. Help us to remember to support each other whenever we are afraid. And help us to remember that we can always turn to you for protection too. Amen

Hymn

No. 41, 'Do Not Be Afraid' in *Mission Praise*, Marshall, Morgan & Scott; or, No. 108, 'The Lord, the Lord is my Shepherd', in *Come and Praise 2*, BBC.

The Starfish Story from South Africa

The aim of this story is to show that whatever we do, or whenever we help someone in desperate need of help, no matter how little or how much we can provide, it can always make a difference to those who are suffering. We cannot help the whole world, but we can help those nearest to us, one at a time.

Begin the story like this.

Sometimes, when faced with huge disasters like the Tsunami, or earthquakes or natural disasters all over the world, or wars, or famine, or drought, or those who need food or shelter or medicines, we are tempted to ask, 'But what can I possibly do, in these circumstances?' Well perhaps this true story about a young boy, can provide some answers. Faced with an impossible task, he still made a huge difference. It is a lesson for all of us.

One day, off the coast of South Africa, an enormous storm blew up. The waves crashed and pounded the beach. Palm tree fronds were ripped from their trees; boats were upturned and flung far away from their moorings; houses were battered and smashed. All night the storm raged and lashed the sea, throwing things up into the air as if they were toys or kites.

In the morning, there was complete peace and calm and stillness and the sun was shining, as if none of the horrors of the night had ever happened. Except that is, for one huge natural disaster that had occurred along the beach.

One little boy, joyful to be alive, crept out of his house near the beach and ran down to inspect the seashore to see what had taken place during the storm. But he was not prepared for what he saw. Tears rolled silently down his cheeks, when he saw the living devastation. The fierceness of the waves had thrown up millions upon millions of helpless, beautiful starfish, all gasping for life, but unable to help themselves to get back into the sea. They were completely stranded and were now beginning to die as the fierce sun pounded them, unmercifully.

The little boy looked about him and asked himself 'What can I possibly do to help all these poor creatures?' Suddenly, he knew what he could do. Painstakingly, one by one, he began throwing each starfish back into the water.

Just then, a man came walking along the beach, also looking at all the devastation and the poor, suffering creatures. Instead of helping the young lad, the man shouted and sneered, 'What on earth do you think you are doing? What difference can you possibly make?'

Undaunted, the little boy called back, 'Quite a lot of difference actually, this one will live', and he continued to throw each starfish back into the water, until his little arms ached. Other people soon came along and seeing his courage and bravery, joined in to help with the unending task.

The teacher needs to draw the threads together and explain that however big the task, and however little we can manage to do, we can still, all make a difference and perhaps by showing our own care, bravery, courage, and positive attitude to do the right thing, we will encourage others to follow our example.

Reflection

Leave a time for quiet reflection, so that the children can think about what they could do today, to make a difference to someone or some situation, in their own small way, to make the world a better place in which to live.

Hymn

No. 79, 'From the Tiny Ant, to the Elephant' in *Come and Praise 2*, BBC.

Prayer

End the assembly with the lovely prayer by Joe Seremane, Field Liaison Officer, Justice and Reconciliation, South African Council of Churches, 'Lord You Asked For My Hands':

> Lord, you asked for my hands that you could use them for your purposes,
> I gave them for a moment and then withdrew – for the work was too hard.
> You asked for my mouth to speak out against injustice;
> I gave you a whisper that I might not be accused.
> You asked for my life that you might work through me;
> I gave you a small part that I might not get too involved.
> Lord, forgive me for calculated efforts to serve you only
> When it is convenient for me to do so;
> Only in places where it is safe to do so;
> Only with those who make it easy for me to do so;
> Father forgive me, renew me and send me out as a usable instrument,
> That I may take seriously the meaning of justice, peace and your cross.
>
> Amen

A Real Christmas

'A Real Christmas' by Elizabeth Peirce was adapted from *The Third Ingredient* by O. Henry.

The aim of the story is to show how sharing with one another is the best gift that we can give to each other. It brings people together and a little can go a very long way to provide happiness for all.

It was Christmas Eve. Jacinta had just plucked her last turkey at the factory where she worked. She had been told by the Foreman to pick up her wages and collect a small gift from the firm. Her poor fingers ached, she had pains in her neck, back and arms from bending over, and plucking the birds in the week before Christmas, ready for other people's Christmas dinner.

Now she looked at her wages and thought, 'It's not very much.' But at least she could pay the rent for her flat. To her delight, the manager shook her by the hand and gave her a small turkey to take home with her, as a leaving present. 'Sorry we can't keep you on after Christmas', he said. 'You've been a good worker, but the work finishes with Christmas – nobody wants turkeys after Christmas.'

Jacinta understood. It was not the first time that she had been made redundant and had had to pound the streets looking for work. 'At least I shall be able to eat this Christmas', she smiled to herself. She was sure that she had some potatoes and vegetables back at the flat, so she need not waste her precious money on non-essentials.

Jacinta's flat was on the fifteenth floor of a huge tenement block. She struggled up the stairs, getting slower and slower and more and more tired. She hardly knew anybody in the block, although she had often smiled at a pretty girl on the fourteenth floor. Letting herself into her flat, Jacinta rushed to the kitchen and looked in the bag where she kept her potatoes and vegetables. NOTHING! Oh, no, absolutely nothing left! How could she eat turkey without roast potatoes and a few vegetables? But she mustn't spend her precious earnings on more food. She still had to pay the rent and the electricity and heating bills. 'Now take hold of yourself', she said sternly to herself. 'At least you have something to eat and, if you are careful, it will last all over Christmas until you can find another job.'

It was then, in a moment of silence, that she heard someone weeping outside. In her haste, she had forgotten to shut the front door and there on the landing was the pretty girl at whom she had often smiled. 'Whatever is the matter?' asked Jacinta kindly. 'My key won't fit the lock', replied the stricken girl, through her tears. 'I'm not surprised', said Jacinta, 'you're on the fifteenth floor, not the fourteenth.' 'I can't be', said the girl, who suddenly realised that she had walked up one flight of stairs too many. She managed a wan smile before bursting into tears again.

'You had better come in and tell me why you are so upset', said Jacinta picking up the girl's shopping bag and parcel. She said her name was Aniya and that she was an artist. The parcel was one of her paintings, which she had been trying to sell so that she could afford to buy food for Christmas. She had taken it to an art gallery, but the manager had laughed at it. He said his cat could have done a better job, painting with its tail! Tragic though it was, both of them managed a weak smile at this. 'So you see,' said Aniya, 'far from being able to buy a small turkey, all I could afford, with the few pence that I have left, was three large potatoes.'

Jacinta made up her mind very quickly. 'Well', she said, 'if you would like to share my small turkey, we could roast your potatoes and we would still have enough to last us through the whole Christmas period.' Aniya suddenly brightened up. 'Are you sure?' she said. 'Quite sure', said Jacinta. 'But I do wish we had some vegetables to go with our meal.' Aniya started weeping again. Jacinta asked her why she was so upset. 'Well, on my way home through the park, I was crying so much that I didn't look where I was going and I slipped and fell into a pond. A kind passer-by jumped into the icy water and rescued me. He dried my legs with his jogging towel, called a taxi, and paid the driver to take me home. I feel so upset because I didn't thank him properly, or even get his name and address so I could write and say thank you.'

Suddenly, there was a crash on the landing followed by a series of minor bumps and crashes. 'Wait here', Jacinta whispered to Aniya, 'I'll go and see what's happened, it's probably my new neighbour who has just moved in opposite me.' Jacinta opened the door cautiously, and sure enough, there was her new neighbour, Sonam, struggling with a pile of parcels. There were vegetables scattered all over the landing floor and halfway down the stairs. 'What are you doing?' asked Jacinta, trying not to eye all the beautiful, fresh vegetables. 'Oh', said Sonam, 'my fingers are all wet and as I was trying to put my key in the door, the paper bags broke and scattered my vegetables all over the place.' Jacinta looked at Sonam more closely, 'It's not just your hands that are wet, you are soaking wet all over. What have you been doing?'

'Well! It's a long story', he said. 'I had been training in the park for an athletics meeting and had forgotten it was Christmas Eve and the shops would be closed tomorrow, so I hadn't bought any food for the holiday period. By the time I remembered and got to the market, everything had been sold. I managed to persuade a stall-holder who was packing up to let me have her last few vegetables. There wasn't any meat left at all.'

'You still haven't told me why you are so wet', said Jacinta. 'Well, I was nearly home', said Sonam, 'when I saw a girl, who wasn't looking where she was going, fall into the pond in the park. I jumped in to rescue her and ended up getting rather wet', he laughed. Jacinta looked at all the lovely vegetables and began to help to pick up sprouts, parsnips, carrots and a swede. She said, 'I don't suppose you would like to share my turkey and my friend's potatoes this Christmas, would you? We haven't got any vegetables and so if we put it all together we could have a fine feast for Christmas.' Sonam smiled from ear to ear. 'I would love to join you and your friend', he said. 'In addition', Jacinta continued, 'I think my friend would like to meet you. Why don't you go and say hello while I pick up the rest of your vegetables?'

Jacinta left the two young people alone together for a moment and then she smiled to herself. It was going to be a lovely Christmas after all!

Prayer

Almighty God, help us this Christmas to think, not so much about what we are going to get, but more about what we can give to others and how we can share whatever we have with those who have nothing. Amen

Hymn

No. 127, 'Christmas Time is Here' in *Come and Praise 2*, BBC.

Reflection

Read the poem below, 'Can Christmas Come for Them?' by John Emery (reproduced with kind permission).

Can Christmas Come for Them?

Shops are full,
    and tinsel bright.
Christmas trees,
    bedecked with light.
Carol Singers,
    in the night,
say Christmas
    comes for them.

Food and drink,
    seem everywhere,
the Church will hold,
    its Christmas Fayre.
Sounds of parties,
    fill the air.
Now Christmas,
    comes for them.

Children's faces,
    all aglow,
watch the Postman,
    come and go.
Bring cards and parcels,
    so they know,
that Christmas,
    comes for them.

In camps a-swarm,
    with desert flies,
children's hunger
    and staring eyes,
say more than
    shouted, strident cries.
Can Christmas
    come for them?

Who might be hungry over Christmas?
What could we do to help?
Discuss sponsoring a child from a developing country. Many organisations such as World Vision operate these schemes. Their address is:

Sponsor a Child
World Vision
Opal Drive
Milton Keynes, MK15 0ZR
Tel: 01908 841010
Web-site: www.worldvision.org.uk

Part 3

Children's Writing About Peace

What Peace/War Means to Me

Start with discussion

What does war and peace mean to individuals? Read one of the story books on page 151 in the resources section, e.g. *Peacetimes* by K. Scholes published by Belitha Press, 1997. Peace means 'a cup of hot chocolate on a winter evening'. Or read *Rose Blanche* by R. Innocenti, published by Red Fox, 2004 (for older children).

Each child will need the following

One piece of drawing paper to make a symbol of peace.
One piece of drawing paper to make an instrument of war.
One piece of writing paper with space for writing 5–10 statements on each side of the paper (depending on the age of the child).
Pencil or pen with which to write.
Felt-tip pens and a selection of collage materials to enhance the drawings.

Make a 'Peace' model for demonstration purposes, e.g. a dove on one side of the paper and an instrument of war on the other side. Then attach a piece of writing paper to the drawing, so that 5–10 statements can be written about what peace means on one side of the paper, and 5–10 statements about what war means on the other side.

For the assembly, choose approximately five children to read their 'Peace' statements and approximately five children to read their 'War' statements. Allow a brief time for discussion/questions from the assembled children. Discuss the merits of peace. Is war ever justified?

End with a simple prayer for peace in our homes, school, the world, perhaps using the children's own words and contributions.

Peace means

1 ----------------------------------

2 ----------------------------------

3 ----------------------------------

4 ----------------------------------

5 ----------------------------------

War means

1 ----------------------------------

2 ----------------------------------

3 ----------------------------------

4 ----------------------------------

5 ----------------------------------

Hymn

No. 144, 'Peace is Flowing like a River'; or No. 145, 'O Let us Spread the Pollen of Peace', both in *Come and Praise 2*, published by the BBC.

Poetry

Read the following three poems: 'Peace', a Buddhist Meditation; 'War' by G. A. Studdert Kennedy; and 'Compassion' by Elizabeth Peirce.

Peace

I am Peace, surrounded by Peace,
secure in Peace.
Peace protects me,
Peace supports me,
Peace is in me,
Peace is mine – all is well.
Peace to all beings
Peace among all beings.
I'm steeped in Peace,
absorbed in Peace.
In the streets, at our work,
having peaceful thoughts,
peaceful words,
peaceful acts.

A Buddhist Meditation

Waste

Waste of Muscle, waste of Brain,
Waste of Patience, waste of Pain,
Waste of Manhood, waste of Health,
Waste of Beauty, waste of Wealth,
Waste of Blood, and waste of Tears,
Waste of youth's most precious years,
Waste of ways the Saints have trod,
Waste of Glory, waste of God –
WAR!

G. A. Studdert Kennedy

Compassion

If in every argument
one person could bend,
there would be an
end to all hostility.
Forgiveness alone would
Turn Hatred into Love,
War into Peace,
Tears into Laughter.
Help me to show this
kind of compassion
rather than revenge.
Silence rather than
angry words,
Love rather than
bitterness.
For peace in the world
must start with me
and how I treat
my friends, neighbours, family.
If only I could show
this unmerited compassion,
Peace could begin again –
from me.

Elizabeth Peirce

A News Report From Bosnia

Meadow and Misha, 'The pain is in my heart'

This is a true story based on a news report from the 1991–1995 war in Bosnia. Fighting had broken out between the Muslims and Serbs who previously had lived happily together for centuries. This press report tells the moving story about a Muslim boy called Meadow and a Serbian soldier called Misha.

Meadow had gone into the hills at night to look for the food for himself and his family that had been dropped by the United Nations aircraft. He went at night, so that he could hide from enemy fire. Meadow took with him whatever implement he could find in the rubble and rubbish of his war-torn city, to use as a torch to light his way and to show him where the food had landed. On this particular occasion, all he could find was some discarded plastic. He set light to this and used it as an improvised torch to search for the food bundles. It was a highly dangerous mission, as Serbian guns were firing all around him trying to prevent the Muslims, like Meadow, from retrieving the food and thus starving them into submission. Meadow's father had already been killed in this tragic task, but Meadow's mother, brothers and sisters were starving. So he pressed on. The plastic torch, however, got out of control quickly and within seconds, as Meadow desperately tried to put it out, his whole body and face caught fire.

Not long afterwards, Meadow was found by a Serbian soldier. He was terrified, fearing the soldier would kill him, and he was in agony from his burns. Surely, he would have died if it had not been for the quick action of the enemy soldier. The soldier, who was called Misha, scooped up Meadow and carried him to the nearest hospital. The surgeon took one look at Meadow and he told the soldier that there was only one way to save the boy's life and that was to give him an immediate skin graft. But who would undergo the painful operation to provide the necessary skin? Without a second's hesitation, Misha himself offered to have the operation to transfer skin from his own legs, to help restore the boy's burnt body and face.

It was this heroic action that saved Meadow's life. After the operation, when the Serbian soldier was asked by the press if he was in any pain from the surgery on his legs, the soldier's answer was simple and sad, 'The pain is not in my legs, but in my heart, I have helped to save a boy's life, that later on, I might have to destroy'.

After telling the above story, open up the whole area of war for discussion.

Points for discussion

1 What do the children know about wars?
2 Why do you think the soldier decided to help the young boy?
3 When the boy was better, do you think his feelings changed towards the enemy soldier? How?

4   What do you think the boy learned from the soldier's actions?
5   What about the soldier's feelings? Do you think that if they ever met again, he could hurt the boy?
6   How much do children know about wars in history? Read the poem below by John Emery, 'Dance in Front of Tanks'. Perhaps plan a visit to the Imperial War Museum in London.
7   Have any of the children, themselves, ever been caught up in war? If so, can they share some of their experiences?
8   Where are there wars going on at the moment? Mark them on a world map or globe. Is there still trouble in the area mentioned in the poem?
9   Having plotted the global wars, count the total number. How many are there?
10 What news reports have the children seen on TV recently? Encourage the children to look for signs of love, hope and peace as in the story.
11 Is there a 'right' side to war?
12 If there is a child in the class who has a parent in the Army, Navy or Airforce, perhaps he/she could be invited to come into school and discuss their peace-keeping role or efforts to prevent wars.
13 Who else, apart from soldiers, gets hurt in wars?
14 Who are refugees? Why do people become refugees?
15 How can the rest of the world help?
16 Could we promote an exchange system between our school and a school in a war-torn area?
17 Could we send supplies, gifts, money, etc. to an area in need?

Dance in Front of Tanks

When democracy is dangled,
Right before a Nation's eyes,
Makes them see what they are missing,
As they almost grasp the prize.
When frustration turns to torrent,
Like a river's flooded banks,
It gave a man the courage once,
To dance in front of tanks.

When a disappointed people,
Watches freedom snatched away.
When they think that they are winning,
And that right will have the day.
But in dawn's ashen light they see,
Their expectations sank,
It drove an ordinary man,
To dance in front of tanks.

Was it bravery or bravado,
As the world was looking on,
Knowing help was not forthcoming,
Realised that hope was gone.
Though he won our admiration,
He deserves his Nation's thanks,
For he showed them his defiance,
As he danced in front of tanks.

We may never ever know his name,
May never learn his fate,
We may never know his motives,
But can only speculate,
On what makes a man a hero,
And lifts him from the ranks,
Yet it happened to a Chinese man,
WHO DANCED IN FRONT OF TANKS.

John J. Emery

(Written at the time of the Tiananmen Square Massacre.
Reproduced with kind permission of the author's daughter. © 1989)

Written work

1   Ask the children to listen to the news, read the daily newspapers and cut out articles on war and peace so that two scrapbooks can be compiled with the researched information; one with war cuttings, the other with peace cuttings.
2   Ask the children to write their own accounts about what they have read; comment on what they have seen, describe their feelings.
3   Encourage the children to keep a diary about a particular (current) war, making daily/weekly entries. Try to encourage the children to look for optimistic signs.
4   Ask the children to imagine what it would be like if their own house and surroundings were bombed, i.e. what would it be like to have no shelter, no water, no food, no security, no medical help, an uncertain future?
5   Let each child write their own suggestions about what he or she could do personally to show that he/she cares for a particular victim/s, i.e. send a message of sympathy to someone, write to a Member of Parliament, collect warm clothes for a particular country, etc.

Share the above research in a joint school assembly. Encourage other classes to contribute to the project. Perhaps combine the assembly with a talk from one of the members of the Armed Forces about their peace-keeping role, or a talk from a member of the Peace Pledge Union, or an activity/talk from Amnesty International (see address and ideas below).

Reflection

Either silence may be kept to think about these things or use the following prayer.

Prayer

Holy God, when we look around at our world today, we seem to see wars everywhere. Help us, your children, to try and bring peace to every situation in which we find ourselves. Help us to take one small step for peace today, in the way we treat each other, our teachers, our families and friends. Help us to be really involved in peace activities. Amen.

Hymn

No. 147, 'Make Me A Channel of Your Peace' in *Come and Praise 2*, BBC.

Amnesty International

17–25 New Inn Yard, London EC2A 3EA
Tel: 02070 331500
Web-site: www.amnesty.org.uk

Information packs, CDs/DVDs, book lists, catalogues, etc. are available. Donations are welcomed for introductory information. Some materials have been especially produced with Primary Schools in mind, other materials are more suitable for Secondary Schools, but the ideas can be adapted. The following packs include:

1   *Rights of the Child*. Exercises for KS 1/2.
2   *The Keys of Freedom Assembly*. A PowerPoint presentation of photographs on CD and a two-minute film about Amnesty International on DVD.
3   *Refugee Voices*. A school assembly for seven voices to go with a PowerPoint presentation on CD. (Can be adapted for KS 2.)
4   *Junior Urgent Action Groups 7–11 years*. Part of Amnesty's worldwide letter-writing campaign on behalf of victims of human rights violations, e.g. victims have included street children in Brazil and Guatemala, child soldiers in Sri Lanka, Sudan and Uganda, young people ill-treated in Romania, Turkey and South Africa, etc.
5   *A list of Speakers* who will come into Schools.
6   *Books* (mainly Secondary, but some Primary).
7   Some *free posters* for Primary Schools.
8   A free booklet containing five activities entitled *Learning About Human Rights Through Citizenship*. Written for Secondary School pupils, the ideas could provide background information for Teachers.

Writing Peace Poems

Rhyme and rhythm, although important, need not be present for a piece of work to be called poetry. Poetry is a personal response, it can be the writer's way of communicating how something affects him or her. Words are very important, especially words that portray a vivid meaning, are 'apt and precise' (*Becoming a Writer Project*, Kent County Council, 1984).

Reading and listening to poetry is of paramount importance to stimulate childrens' own creative writing. As with the descriptive writing mentioned on page 81, the Teacher could try and encourage sensory awareness in a piece of poetry writing; the use of similies; alliteration; resonance and imagery, etc.

Teachers may like to encourage children to write their own poetry about peace, utilising all the freshness and originality that children can bring to their work, before trying out the idea given below. The idea is offered only as a starting point, but it is important to avoid stereotyping children's work and so it may be better if the approach suggested is only used after other ideas have been explored first. However, this approach was used successfully with American primary school children and the results are published in a book entitled *Peace Poems by Children* edited by Mary Rudge and published by Artists Embassy International, 50 Oak Street, San Francisco CA 94102, 1983. (This is one of the books in the British Poetry Library, see address below.)

The idea described in this book is to make up one's own poem using the initial letters of a word, e.g. P E A C E. (Below is the author's attempt.)

PEACE

P eople matter,

E veryone can be loved.

A sk God for His peace.

C ostly love brings peace,

E verlasting peace.

For the assembly, children can either read their own efforts aloud to the assembled children or the Teacher could act as Scribe and create an instant poem on the theme of Peace, using the ideas given by children and staff from the floor.

End the assembly with a time of quiet reflection on the created poem/s.

Hymn

No. 497, 'My Peace I Give Unto You' in *Mission Praise* published by Marshall Pickering.

Useful address

The British Poetry Library
Level 5, Royal Festival Hall
South Bank Centre
London SE1 8XX
Tel: 02079 210943 / Fax: 02079 210939
e-mail: poetrylibrary@rfh.org.uk
web-site: www.poetrylibrary.org.uk

Membership is free and a whole range of services are provided for schools, pupils and teachers. In-service days can be arranged; books, tapes, videos, CDs and 'Poetry Sacks' (books, activities, masks and instruments for 5–9 year olds) can be freely borrowed. Free book lists, information about special events, magazines, publishers, and competition lists are also available. Contact the library to arrange a visit.

Poetry

Read the poem 'Peace' by Frank Topping.

Peace

A friend asked me,
'If you were granted one wish,
what would you ask for?'
And I said, 'Peace, world peace;
peace in the heart
of every man, woman and child.'
For thousands of years
people have dreamed
of the day when the lamb
would lie down with the lion,
and swords would be made
into ploughshares.
But an end to all conflict
would mean the end of sin;
so is the wish an impossible dream?
Is peace an impossible dream?

Today, from a train
rushing towards the city
I caught a glimpse of fields
rich with crops.
I saw a stream,
meandering slowly
beside tree-lined banks,
leaves rustling over gentle water.

As we slowed for Stone Cross Halt,
even from the train
I could hear birds singing –
summer birds
who had, yet again
made the impossible journey
of thousands of miles.
We live in a beautiful world,
and the impossible
happens all the time.
Fields and streams can be peaceful,
but peace is not a place –
it is a state of mind
in a particular man or woman.
And world peace
has to begin with individual people:
peace within ourselves;
peace within our families;
peace in all our relationships.
Perhaps, for my wish
I should have asked
for peace within myself,
because, perhaps world peace –
begins with me.

Pentecost and a Yucky Fruit Cake

Today's assembly is about helping children to understand what Pentecost means in practical terms. The information is based on the first Pentecost, as it is recorded in Acts Chapter 2, in the Bible. It describes the first coming of the Holy Spirit. The practical outworking of what this means today can best be understood by reading Galatians Chapter 5: 22–23. These verses tell us what it means to have the fruits of His Holy Spirit in our lives, i.e. love, joy, peace, patience, kindness, goodness, faithfulness, gentleness and self-control. This is what Jesus promised to all those who ask.

The first coming of Jesus' Spirit occurred ten days after He had ascended into Heaven. This was fifty days after His Resurrection. Pentecost, which is also the name of the festival, is the Greek word meaning fiftieth. Acts describes how all the disciples were gathered together in one room, when suddenly there was the sound of rushing wind and it appeared as if 'tongues of fire' were resting above each of the disciples' heads and they began to speak in different languages. Peter told everyone that it was the coming of the Holy Spirit, just as Jesus had promised, then and for all time in the future. He would give His Holy Spirit to all those who asked him and said they were sorry for their sins. He would replace all their 'yuckiness' with good things like love, joy, patience, etc. Of course, we would have to ask for these fruits every day, as we so often go wrong. But His Spirit would enable people to become more like Him, to understand the Bible, to pray effectively and to help change their behaviour.

Begin with two readings from the Bible: Galatians Chapter 5: 22–23 (the list of fruits) and Jeremiah 17: 10 'I the Lord search the heart and examine the mind' (RSV). Then act the following drama called 'Yucky Fruit Cakes' and include a third reading, Mathew 23: 25–28 about what one looks like on the outside, but also what is going on inside.

You will need the following props

Chef's hat and apron
Empty cake box with a picture of a lovely cake on the outside
Large dirty mixing bowl
175 grams of flour mixed with earth
Sugar bag containing pebbles
Milk that is clearly 'off'
Two bad eggs that smell
Over-sized reading glasses and recipe
Large black bin bag to put the mixture in at the end!
Nine 'Fruits of the Spirit' on flash cards to be held up

Begin the drama in the following way. Emphasise what a good Cook you are because you are putting on your *chef's hat and apron* and that this will turn you into an 'expert' because you *look* the part.

Hold up the *cake box* for all to see and tell the children that you are going to show them how to make a wonderful cake exactly like the one on the box. Put on the *oversized reading glasses* and take out the *recipe*. (Could be a bunch of computer paper that falls to the ground as you read out the ingredients.) Then say:

Oh this looks easy peasy. Let's see, I need the recipe – and my reading glasses – I don't want to make a mistake. (*Put the glasses on*)

Now I need my mixing bowl. Oh dear it's a bit dirty, I think that's a bit of spaghetti stuck to the side. Never mind, I'm sure it won't matter. At least it's not alphabetti-spaghetti. (*Show the dirty inside of the bowl.*)

175 grams of flour (+ dirt). Umm the flour looks a bit yucky. Do you think it's alright? Oh! I think it will be fine. (*Tip black mixture into bowl.*)

175 grams of sugar. Now that's a nuisance, I forgot to buy any more sugar. But I do have a few stones in my sugar-bag. Well, they both begin with S, don't they? Sugar, Stones. I'm sure they will do, it is probably the correct *weight* that counts, not what's inside the bag. (*Add to bowl.*)

Milk – sniff, pooh this smells awful. I think it's gone off. (*Tip into mixture.*)

Eggs – pooh! Pooh! Oh dear these smell rotten. But in they go. (*Break shells and add to cake.*)

Now the recipe says mix everything together – so here we go. (*Make a show of mixing.*)

(*Walk amongst the assembled children to show the mixture, stirring as you go.*)

Anyone want a taste?

Who would like to lick the bowl? (There is always one bright spark who says 'yes'. Tell them they can eat it *all* later!)

Based on an idea given to me by a friend. Origin unknown.

Now ask a child to read Jesus' words in Mathew 23: 25–28:

Woe to you, teachers of the law and Pharisees, you hypocrites! You clean the outside of the cup and dish, but inside they are full of greed and self-indulgence. Blind Pharisee! First clean the inside of the cup and dish, and then the outside also will be clean. (NIV)

I wonder what Jesus meant?

(*Produce the cake box again.*) I think Jesus was saying that we take a lot of trouble with the outward appearance of things, when it is what is going on inside that really matters and makes something good.

What makes a good cake is good ingredients, not just what it looks like on the box. I think that is what Jesus meant. And it is the same with us. Not just what we look like on the outside, but we need a few good ingredients inside. Just as bad ingredients make a bad cake – bad things can spoil us. We need good things going on inside to make us into beautiful people.

We have to begin by clearing away the rubbish and start again. (*Sweep contents of cake + bowl into the black bin bag.*)

First of all we need to ask Jesus to forgive us for all our nastiness and ask Him to give us His Spirit. Micah Chapter 7 Verse 19 says he will take all our sins and hurl them into the depths of the sea, where they will be forgiven and forgotten.

Now what good ingredients do we need inside us? (*Ask a child to read Galatians 5: 22–23 again.*) So we need these good fruits inside us. Then we shall become lovely fruit cakes rather than yucky cakes.

Go through the list, asking nine children to hold up the words on the cards as you mention them.

Love – that is making friends and being loving
Joy – making other people laugh, having fun
Peace – not fighting
Patience – waiting our turn
Kindness – being helpful
Goodness – looking after others
Faithfulness – or trust in Jesus
Gentleness – Proverbs 15 says: 'A gentle word turns away anger'
Self-control – not always arguing or losing your temper

End the assembly by asking the children to reflect on how they could be lovely fruit cakes rather than yucky ones, or use the following prayer:

Prayer

Dear Jesus, we are sorry for all the wrong things we do. Help us to be more like you. Help us to demonstrate the fruits of your Spirit. Give us love, joy, peace, patience, kindness, goodness, faithfulness, gentleness and self-control in our lives, so that we can make our homes, our schools and our environments, better places to live in. Amen

Hymn

No. 92, 'When God the Holy Spirit Came down on Whitsunday' in *Infant Praise*, published by Oxford University Press.

Further development

Ask the children to write about how they could demonstrate each of the fruits. For example, Love: 'I am Love, I try to love my brothers and sisters. I try to express my love for other children in need, by giving some of my pocket money. Jesus said, "Love your neighbour as yourself". I am learning to love a person I find difficult.'

Now read the poem 'Love' by Elizabeth Peirce.

Love

I read somewhere long ago
of a lady who kissed
the gaping hole in a leper's face.
This surely was love?

I heard a young girl
giving her seat on the bus
to an old woman, tired and worn.
I think this probably was love.

I watched an old man planting
trees, picking up litter
for the ease of others.
I reckoned this might be love.

I turned and saw a small child
giving his sandwiches
to a beggar, huddled and befuddled
on the corner of our street.
This had to be love.

Then I saw it all clearly,
it was sacrifice of self
that underpinned all these
and I know at last,
that this is love.

Elizabeth Peirce

Laughter is the Best Medicine

Anyone who has ever felt a bit depressed, cross or irritable will know that laughter can often break tension. It is hard to keep a straight face when everyone about you is splitting their sides. It is amazing how quickly goodwill and good humour can spread as a result of having a good laugh or trying to see the funny side of a situation. Therefore, in an assembly book about peace, it is a legitimate topic for school worship.

First of all, some discussion should take place about different types of laughter. For instance, when is it rude to laugh, or can you hurt someone by laughing? Should you laugh at another's misfortune? When is it acceptable? Having agreed some principles, the assembly could be a time to really enjoy some funny experiences. One way to begin, is to read the following poem 'Daddy Fell Into the Pond', by Alfred Noyes in *Here We Go Poems* selected by S. Mclellar and published by Evans Bros. Ltd., 1982.

Daddy Fell Into the Pond

Everyone grumbled. The sky was grey.
We had nothing to do and nothing to say.
We were nearing the end of a dismal day.
And there seemed to be nothing beyond,
    Then
        Daddy fell into the pond!

And everyone's face grew merry and
    bright,
And Timothy danced for sheer delight.
Give me the camera, quick, oh quick!
He's crawling out of the duckweed!' Click!

Then the gardener suddenly slapped his
    knee,
And doubled up, shaking silently,
And the ducks all quacked as if they were
    daft,
And it sounded as if the old drake
    laughed.
Oh, there wasn't a thing that didn't
    respond
When
    Daddy fell into the pond!

Perhaps some children or staff could be persuaded to tell or write or draw a few jokes. (Although these may need to be carefully vetted beforehand!) Or a class could dress up as clowns and perform some rolling, tumbling, tripping-up feats. For a real treat, perhaps a video of a funny TV programme could be shown. Sequences showing pets doing funny things are always popular. Often parents have camcorders and videos of their own and may be willing to share their own funny moments with the rest of the school. When everyone has had a really good laugh, end with a simple prayer of thanks to God, for all the happiness and joy that we can share when we laugh.

Hymns

No. 14, 'Stand Up, Clap Hands, Shout Thank You, Lord', in *Someone's Singing Lord*, published by A & C Black; or No. 4, 'O Lord! Shout For Joy!' in the same book; or No. 98, 'You Shall Go Out With Joy and Be Led Forth With Peace', in *Come and Praise 2*, published by the BBC.

Poetry

The assembly can be brought to a close with the final poem entitled 'Smile'.

Smile

A smile costs nothing but gives much,
It enriches those who receive,
Without making poorer those who give,
It takes but a moment,
But the memory lasts forever.
None is so rich or mighty that he can get
  along without it,
And none is so poor that he can't be
  made rich by it.
A smile creates happiness in the home,
Fosters good will in business,
And is the countersign of friendship.
It brings rest to the weary,
Cheer to the discouraged,
Sunshine to the sad.
It is nature's best antidote for
  trouble,
Yet it cannot be bought, begged,
  borrowed or stolen,
For it is something that is of no value to
  anyone
until it is given away.
Some people are too tired to smile,
Give them one of yours,
As none needs a smile so much,
As he who has no more to give.

(Origin unknown)

Address

Pauline Books and Media produce lots of lovely celebratory posters.
199 Kensington High Street
London W8 6BA
Tel: 02079 379591 Fax: 02079 379910
e-mail: london@pauline-uk.org
web-site: www.pauline-uk.org/posters

Peace Verses in the Bible

This assembly will need a great deal of preparation beforehand. Each child will need a bible. The children could work in groups. Three or four concordances are needed or a computer Study Bible (such as those available from Sunrise Software, PO Box 300, Carlisle, Cumbria CA3 0QS. Tel: 08450 579579; fax: 01228 514949; web-site: www.sunrise-software.com).

Each group leader looks up the word 'Peace' in the concordance or on the computer and then gives each of the children in his/her group a reference to research in their own bibles. Different group leaders could be given different sections of the bible, i.e. the Old or New Testaments or the Psalms or Proverbs, Isaiah or Kings, etc. For example, five children can look up the references in Psalms. What do the Psalms say about Peace?

(Quotations, unless stated otherwise are from The Good News Bible published by the Bible Societies/HarperCollins Publishers Ltd, UK, © American Bible Society 1966, 1971, 1976, 1992, 1994. Used with permission. RSV quotations are used with permission of The National Council of the Churches of Christ in the USA.)

Psalm 29: 11   The Lord gives strength to his people and blesses them with peace
Psalm 34: 14   Turn away from evil and do good, strive for peace with all your heart.
Psalm 85: 10   Righteousness and peace will kiss each other (RSV)
Psalm 120: 71   I am for peace (RSV)
(*There are many more*)

Or what does it say in the Gospels?

Matthew 5: 9   Blessed are the peacemakers, for they shall be called sons of God (RSV)
Mark 9: 50   Live in peace with one another
John 14: 27   Peace I leave with you, my peace I give to you (RSV)
John 16: 33   In me you may have peace (NIV)

The children could either make their own book of 'Peace' sayings or illustrate their particular reference and give an explanation of what it means. These can be presented in an assembly, with each child holding up his or her work and telling the rest of the school what they have learnt.

The idea can be extended to include 'Peace' sayings from other sources. For instance, Anne Frank said, 'I still believe that people are really good at heart . . . If I look into the Heavens, I think that it will come out right and that peace and tranquillity will return again.' Of course, much research is needed by the children, first. Who was Anne Frank, how could she say something about peace in her dreadful circumstances? Perhaps the children could visit the Anne Frank Touring Exhibition, or read about her life story. (See addresses for information on pages 21–22).

Other sources to be researched could include the sayings of the leaders of the World Faiths. For instance, the Buddha, or Muhammad, or some of the 'Tales of the Hasidim'. The sayings of modern day giants, such as the black mother Gee Walker, who astounded her hearers by saying that she forgave the murderers of her beloved son when he was stabbed in the park in 2005. There are many useful books to help you in the *Some People of Peace* Resources section on pages 62–63.

Peace resources for teachers

Ansell, J. *et al.*, *Prayers for Peacemakers*, Kevin Mayhew Ltd., 1988.

Ferguson, J., *Give Peace a Chance*, Gooday Publishers, 1988.

Hussey, M., *Anne Frank Declaration*, The Anne Frank Ed. Trust, 2000 (*Guidelines for Teachers to Prepare an Assembly*).

Masheder, M., *Let's Play Together*, Green Print, 1989 (over 300 co-operative games).

Pax Christi, *Peacemaking, Day by Day*, Russell Press, 1990 (daily readings).

Rearden, J. (ed.), *Leaves From the Tree of Peace*, United Reform Church, 1986 (also has a set of slides to accompany the poems).

Rearden, J. (ed.), *Threads of Creation* (+ slides), United Reform Church, 1989.

Smith, P. D., *Peace Offerings*, Stainer and Bell, 1986.

Poetry

Read the peace poem by Jill Arthur in *Voices Speaking Peace* compiled by E. Birtles, published by The Unitarian Peace Fellowship, 1990 (used with kind permission of the author).

Peace is Not the Absence of War

Peace is not the absence of war,
peace is so much more;
peace comes from the inner being,
touching, knowing, seeing.
There is only one way peace can be taught
and that is living as we ought,
with peace in every word we say –
in all we do, come what may.

Some People of Peace

A Hindu Story for Jagannath's Rathayatra (or 'The Lord of the Universe's Chariot Journey')

Jagannath means Lord (nath) of the Universe (jagan). Rathayatra means chariot (rath, pronounced 'rut'); journey (yatra). Usually the festival of Jagannath's Rathayatra takes place in July (although the date does change), when an image of Jagannath and his brother and sister is placed on a huge chariot and pulled through the streets. Many Hindus will take a turn in pulling the chariot as part of their duty and to share in the blessing of Jagannath. Prashad or food that has been offered to God is shared amongst the festival goers.

> Once upon a time a long time ago, there lived a devout King, who wanted to find God and to serve him. One day, a pilgrim who had travelled many miles came to the King's court and told the King that, at last, the pilgrim had found God living on top of a mountain a long way away.
>
> Immediately, the King became very excited and wanted to go and find God for himself. But he decided to send his Chief Priest first, to find the place and to see if the pilgrim's story was true.
>
> The Chief Priest set off and travelled the long distance, until at last he came to the special mountain top of which the pilgrim had spoken. He found a group of very poor people living and working there and worshipping God. The Priest persuaded these humble people to show him the special, peaceful place where God could be found.
>
> Reluctantly, the people agreed, but only if the Priest agreed to be blindfolded, so that he could not find his way back there, so that the place would remain undisturbed by lots of visitors. The Priest agreed, but remembering his promise to the King to show him the location, he took along with him in his hand some tiny mustard seeds, which he dropped silently along the path as they went along. He knew that the seeds would sprout up and grow, and he would be able to retrace his steps and find his way back again by following the trail. He did indeed find God and so set off back home to tell the King what he had found and how he would be able to find the special place again.
>
> Very soon the mustard seeds sprouted and grew all along the path to God's special place. So the King and the Chief Priest set off back to the mountain. They carefully followed the

path, by looking for the mustard plants all along the way. They found the exact place and then waited patiently for God to appear. But although they waited and waited for many days, God did not appear.

However, it was in this peaceful place that the King was told that God would appear, if he built a huge temple in which all could worship. So the King set about employing many craftsmen to construct a beautiful temple in which they could all worship Jagannath (or God) together. But even when the temple was built, Jagannath did not appear.

The King then learned that God's image would be imprinted on a special piece of wood. Once more, the King waited and waited, but still God's image did not appear. Many years later, the King had a very strange dream. He dreamt that the special piece of wood for which he had been searching was beside a distant seashore, floating in the sea.

So once again he set off with all his servants and retainers to find this piece of wood. To his delight he found the wood, but none of his servants could lift it. They harnessed up the King's elephants to pull the wood out of the sea, but yet again, the wood would not budge. Just then, a Holy Man called a Swami appeared and he lifted the wood out of the water, with such ease, as if it were a twig.

So the King ordered his carpenters to carve the image of Jagannath, the Lord of the Universe. But the carpenters had to admit defeat. They found that they could not carve the wood at all, it was too hard. Once again, to the King's delight, the Swami reappeared. He told the King that he would carve the Lord's image if he was left alone to do so.

For five days and five nights, the Holy Man carved Jagannath's image. But the King became very impatient and broke his promise not to disturb the Swami, and he rushed in to see what the image of God looked like. But the Swami had vanished and the carving was incomplete. It had no hands or feet.

The King was terribly disappointed, until one day, reading one of his ancient books, he discovered that it said 'God has no hands or feet'. And the King realised at last, that even without hands or feet, God is still able to bless us every day and we can be God's hands and feet and bless others too.

'This story reminds Hindus that their search for God may take a long time, and that no image can ever really show what God is like'.

Adapted from the version which appears in *Listening to Hindus* by Robert Jackson and Eleanor Nesbitt published by Unwin Hyman Ltd., 1990, page 18.

Reflection

In a moment of quiet think how you can bring blessing to others today.

Hymn

No. 94, 'Make Us Worthy Lord to Serve Our Fellow Men' in *Come and Praise 2*, BBC.

Hindu prayer

By your favours granted, enable us, O Lord,
Once again to leap over the pitfalls that face us.
Be a high tower, powerful and broad,
for both us and our children.
To our people bring well-being and peace.

From Rig Veda 1, 189

Bob Geldof and People of Peace
Topic Book

Opening scene: The Queen of England, Her Royal Highness Queen Elizabeth II, knights Bob Geldof, 'Arise, Sir Robert Geldof.'

How did this extraordinary knighthood come about for a scruffy, long-haired, outspoken pop-singer?

Perhaps one of Bob Geldof's recordings could be played in the assembly, i.e. 'I don't like Mondays'. Then the teacher needs to explain that this young man, who did not like school very much, was often rude and difficult, raised over seventy million pounds for the starving millions in Africa.

If this assembly is to be used to launch the children's own topic books on 'People of Peace', then they need to be given a few guidelines:

1 First draw up a brief historical overview of the chosen person. For example:

   (i)   Robert Geldof was born in Dublin, Ireland, on the 5th October 1954.
   (ii) His mother died when he was only five years old.
   (iii) In 1975, Bob became the lead singer of a pop group called 'The Boomtown Rats'.
   (iv) In October 1984, when Bob was 30 years old and his pop-singing career was not going very well, he saw the terrible pictures on the television of the people starving in Ethiopia.
   (v)   In less than a month, he decided to make the record 'Do they know it's Christmas?' which he co-wrote with Midge Ure of 'Ultravox' in order to send the proceeds to the famine relief. He started to ring all the pop groups that he knew, to ask them to help, including Ultravox, Sting, Duran Duran, Spandau Ballet, Boy George, Frankie Goes to Hollywood, Style Council, etc. The date of the recording for the Band Aid record was set for Sunday 25th November 1984.
   (vi) Bob then got as much publicity as he could by phoning newspapers, television companies, etc. In two weeks the record raised five million pounds for the starving people in Ethiopia. Then Bob had to go to Africa to see how the money should be spent. He met Heads of Governments, Aid Agencies and all the people who were trying to help on the ground.
   (vii) Bob realized that a lot more money was needed. There was starvation right across Northern Africa and not just in Ethiopia, but also in Sudan, Chad, Niger and Mali. He thought of doing an even bigger fund-raising event, a 'Live Aid Concert' at Wembley Stadium in London which would be seen across the world. He decided to involve bands from all over the world simultaneously to raise funds for the twenty million starving people in Africa. He

contacted bands in America, Australia, Germany, Holland, Russia and Japan and asked them to be involved in the concert. He telephoned TV companies, airlines, telephone companies and the police to ask them to give their services free of charge. He invited the Prince and Princess of Wales. The date of the Live Aid Concert was set for 13th July 1985. Appeals for money from the general public were made. The money kept coming in and by the end of the year, sixty-six million pounds had been collected.

(viii) Once again, Bob returned to Africa to see how the money should be spent. He spoke to Governments, the European Parliament, the Australian Government, etc. Other aid funds were started, i.e. Fashion Aid, School Aid, Sports Aid, etc. The money was used to buy food, clothes, medicines, to build schools, clinics, houses, etc. It was given to small farmers to enable them to buy seeds, animals, trees and machinery.

(ix) On the 24th July 1986, the Queen made Bob Geldof a knight: 'Sir Robert Geldof'.

2 The second part of the topic book could include geographical locations.

(i) These could be plotted and then traced on a world map. First, where the main character was born, i.e. in this example, Bob Geldof was born in Dublin, Ireland.

(ii) Second, his travels across the world could be plotted, i.e. Bob went across the Northern States of Africa, but he also went to America, Australia, the European Parliament, etc.

3 In the third part, the topic book could include some of the famous people that the main character encountered and a brief account of what they said to each other. For example, Bob met:

The Queen
The Prince and Princess of Wales
Mother Teresa
Margaret Thatcher
Heads of Governments
Heads of Universities
Heads of Industries

4 Fourth, the topic book could include any photographs, newspaper cuttings and memorabilia that the children can find.

5 Finally, the children could be encouraged to write a bibliography.

Prayer

How can we have peace, Lord, when half the world is starving? Thank you for people like Bob Geldof who try and help countless millions. Bless their work. Help us to be ready to help in whatever way we can. Help us to share, give and go on giving, so that others can have their basic needs met. Amen.

Hymn

No. 74, 'Sad, Puzzled Eyes of Small Hungry Children' in *Come and Praise 2*, BBC.

Books about Bob Geldof

Gray, C., *Bob Geldof: The Pop Star Who Raised 70 Million Pounds for Famine Relief in Ethiopia*, Exley Publications Ltd., 1987
May, C., *Bob Geldof*, Hamish Hamilton, 1988.

Further books for children to use in their research topic book 'People of Peace' are listed in 'Resources', below.
Now read the poem 'Giving' by Elizabeth Peirce.

Giving

It's funny when buying the latest
computer game or Doc Marten shoes,
Ten pounds or more seems too little.
Yet when the man on TV
was asking me to give
Ten pounds to help some child overseas,
It seemed too much.
What a funny world we live in
When half the human race
cannot keep pace 'cos
they're starving.
And I can't eat my beans and chips,
seems something's wrong somewhere,
as if we don't care for anyone else but us.
My mum says she can't understand,
what's all the fuss,
as long as she can have her bottle of wine
and guests to dine
and is there enough cream
for the pud?
But I've got a feeling
that the man appealing on TV
had a point.
We should all be giving
and go on giving
until all the world's children
has even one pair of shoes.
And has enough food
so the man on the news is redundant.

Elizabeth Peirce (1995)

Resources

Anne Frank House, *The World of Anne Frank*, Macmillan Children's Books, 2003 (a photographic history with clear captions).
Benson, M., *Nelson Mandela*, Hamish Hamilton, 1986.
du Boulay, S., *Changing the Face of Death: The Story of Dame Cecily Saunders*, RMEP (Chansitor), 2000.

Claybourne, A., *Martin Luther King*, Hodder Wayland, 2002.

Comerford, P., *Desmond Tutu: Black Africa's Man of Destiny*, St Paul Publications, 1988.

Constant, A., *In the Streets of Calcutta: Story of Mother Teresa*, RMEP (Chansitor), 1999.

Constant, A., *Man of Peace: Story of Mahatma Gandhi*, RMEP (Chansitor), 1998.

Godwin, S., *A Sword for Joan of Arc*, Hodder Wayland, 2000.

Hanks, G., *City of Darkness: Story of Jackie Pullinger*, RMEP (Chansitor), 1998.

Hanks, G. and Owen, R. J., *In His Service: The Stories of Martin Luther King, Father Damien, Trevor Huddleston, Jackie Pullinger and Dr. Barnardo*, RMEP (Chansitor), 1991 (Book 3 in series, suitable for 11+ aged children).

Hanks, G. and Owen, R. J., *In His Service: The Stories of Mother Teresa, Chad Varah, Corrie Ten Boom, Helen Keller, William Booth*, RMEP (Chansitor), 1993 (Book 1 in series).

Hanks, G. and Owen, R. J., *In His Service: The Stories of David Wilkinson, Nicky Cruz, Brother Andrew, Stanley Browne, Gladys Aylward*, RMEP (Chansitor), 1994 (Book 2 in the series, suitable for 11+ aged children).

Hussey, M., *Anne Frank Declaration: Guidelines for Teachers*, Anne Frank Ed. Trust, 2000.

Johnson, E., *Mother Teresa*, Franklin Watts, 2003.

Mackenzie, C., *Mary Slessor: Servant to the Slave*, Christian Focus Pub., 2000.

Maddison, L. and Messina, C., *Joan of Arc*, Random House, 1999.

Malam, J., *Mary Seacole*, Evans Bros., 2004.

Owen, R. J., *Free at Last: Story of Martin Luther King*, RMEP (Chansitor), 1998.

Poole, J. and Barret, B., *Anne Frank*, Hutchinson, 2005. (Beautiful illustrations, capturing the historical feel, yet depicting Anne as a normal little girl with her family and friends, a bit naughty at school! Moving on to wearing the yellow star; her forced hiding from the Nazis and her eventual heart-breaking capture. Useful chronology of events at the back of the book. Only one criticism, the print size of the chronology is far too small.)

Maximilian Kolbe

The power of love is stronger than the power of hate.

Children need to know that any form of racism is wrong and cannot be tolerated. Daily, in the media, we read about one race trying to exterminate another race. We hear that despicable phrase 'ethnic cleansing' and we see examples of fanatics showing hatred towards a people of a different religion, race or culture.

But the power of love is stronger than the power of hate and when good is seen to triumph, somehow a single act is remembered down the years.

Jesus said, 'Greater love has no man than this, that a man lay down his life for his friends' (John 15: 13. RSV).

Auschwitz was a monument to hate where people were gassed, shot, tortured, humiliated and starved to death. The film *Schindler's List*, although unsuitable for primary school children, would give the teacher a very clear insight into the tremendous suffering of the Jewish people, and there is a very real need for this message to be spread from generation to generation to prevent such racism ever happening again.

Maximilian Kolbe's story is one way of introducing the subject of the Holocaust to junior school children and shows love triumphing over hatred. There were countless other acts of love even in that hateful place of Auschwitz (see also p. 18), but Maximilian's life would be an appropriate story for children to research, since much has been written about him. His actions also provide a suitable entry point for the whole discussion of the Holocaust

Briefly, the outline of Maximilian Kolbe's life and acts of love are these:

1   Maximilian was a Franciscan Priest, who published newspapers from his Monastery in Poland during the Second World War. When this was not allowed by the Nazi authorities, the Franciscan Brothers helped refugees. They looked after the sick and did anything they could to relieve the suffering of the local people.

2   Hitler decided that not only should all Jews be exterminated, but all Priests should be exterminated too. So on the 17th of February 1941 Maximilian and five Priests were taken to Pawiak Prison in Warsaw by the Gestapo. On the 28th of May 1941, the prisoners were loaded onto cattle trucks and sent on the train to Auschwitz.

3   Taken through the electrified barbed-wire fences of the camp (which meant instant death to anyone who touched them), past the watchtowers with their searchlights and machine-guns and into the reception block, the prisoners' heads were shaved and they were issued with prison caps, blue and white striped tunics

and trousers and wooden clogs. The prisoners were given numbers which were tattooed on their forearms. Maximilian's number was 16670.

4   The prisoners slept on wooden bunks, given meagre rations and forced to work on whatever project the Nazis wanted. Most were beaten, tortured or gassed. There were many stories about Maximilian's kindnesses whilst in Auschwitz. He often gave away his soup, he looked after those who were sick and prayed for those who asked for his prayers and absolution. He taught his fellow prisoners that hatred was destructive but love was creative.

5   Once, the Nazi in charge of Maximilian's work-detail forced Maximilian to run at double the pace carrying heavy loads on his back. When Maximilian finally collapsed he was beaten nearly to death.

6   In July, after Maximilian had been in Auschwitz for nearly two months, one of the prisoners in his block went missing. The Second-in-Command, a man called Fritzsch, ordered that ten men would be starved to death as a punishment for the whole block. At roll call, Fritzsch chose ten men at random to die this slow and painful death. Francis Gajowniczck, who was one of the ten chosen, cried out in despair that he would never see his wife or children again. It was at this point that Maximilian stepped forward and said 'I am a Polish Catholic Priest. I am old. I want to take his place, because he has a wife and children.' Fritzsch, surprisingly, allowed Maximilian to die instead of Gajowniczck.

7   The prisoners were taken to Block 11, known as Death Block, stripped of their clothing and slowly starved to death. A prisoner who worked in Death Block and who survived the war described what he saw and heard. Every day, instead of cries of despair and hatred and curses, he heard hymn singing and loving prayers led by Maximilian. After two weeks five prisoners had died, but five prisoners, including Maximilian, were still alive, so the S. S. finally killed them all by injecting them with poison. Yet Maximilian's life had not been in vain, he had fulfilled the words of Jesus right to the end of his life; 'Greater love has no man than this, that a man lay down his life for his friends.'

Reflection

Today in his cell, an eternal flame is kept alight to show that goodness triumphs over evil. Leave a time to reflect on this and also guide the children's thinking, by reminding them that anti-racist attitudes, bullying, etc. is never right.

Prayer

Or read the following prayer, scribbled on a piece of paper, found near a dead child at Ravensbruck Concentration Camp.

O Lord, remember those of ill-will,
but do not remember all the suffering
they inflicted on us;
Remember the fruits we have bought
thanks to our suffering –

our comradeship, our loyalty,
our humility, our courage,
our generosity, the greatness of heart
which has grown out of all this . . .

Song

Sing the lovely Jewish Traditional Song, 'Kol Ha Olam Kulo'. Words and music below. (For pronunication guide to words, see page 19).

Kol Ha Olam Kulo

Kol ha olam kulo gesher tzar m'od,
gesher tzar m'od, gesher tzar m'od.
Kol ha olam kulo gesher tzar m'od
gesher tzar m'od.
V'ha'ikar, v'ha'ikar
Lo l'fahed, lo l'fahed klal
V'ha'ikar, v'ha'ikar.
Lo l'fahed klal.

The whole world is like a narrow bridge and the essential thing is never to be afraid.

Angela Wood says, 'this is a famous Hasidic dictum which fits Yom Ha Shoah very well as a testimony to both vulnerability and courage'.

Hymns

No. 140, 'Lead Me From Death To Life'; or No. 146, 'We Ask That We Live And Labour in Peace', both in *Come and Praise* 2, published by the BBC.

Poem

Read the poem 'First They Came for the Jews', by Pastor Martin Niemoller (1892–1984). He was imprisoned for seven years in Sachenhausen and Dachau Concentration Camps.

First They Came for the Jews

First they came for the Jews
and I did not speak out –
because I was not a Jew.
Then they came for the communists
and I did not speak out –
because I was not a communist.
Then they came for the trade unionists
and I did not speak out –
because I was not a trade unionist.
Then they came for me –
and there was no one left
to speak out for me.

Useful addresses

For information about *Schindler's List*, write to:

Film Education
21–22 Poland Street
London W1F 8QQ
Tel: 02078 519450
Fax: 02074 393218
e-mail: postbox@filmeducation.org
web-site: www.filmeducation.org

Also for a *Schindler's List* free guide contact:
The Southern Institute for Education and Research
Mailing address: 31 McAlister Drive
New Orleans, LA 70118
Tel: (504) 865–6100
Fax: (504) 862–8026
e-mail: so-inst@tulane.ed
web-site: www.southerninstitute.info/holocaust_education/schind.html

Rosa Parks and Martin Luther King

No assembly book on Peace would be complete without some mention of the inspiring 1964 Nobel Peace Prize Winner, Martin Luther King.

All children can learn from his great example that racial discrimination (that is, treating those of a different race from one's own in an inferior way) or segregation (that is, separating one minority group from another group) is wrong and cannot be tolerated.

Many parts of Martin Luther King's life story could be chosen and dramatised for a school assembly, or researched for an individual topic book (part of his famous 'I Have a Dream' speech is included below).

But the part that has been chosen for this assembly is the Rosa Parks incident that set Martin Luther King on his quest for Civil Rights for all black people in America.

The play can be rehearsed briefly before the assembly or mimed as the teacher reads the story.

You will need the following characters

Martin Luther King
Rosa Parks
Bus Driver
Chief of Police
Rev Ralph Abernathy
Crowd of black people
Narrator

You will need the following props

Chairs (arranged like seats on a bus)
Bus Driver's outfit
Police outfit and handcuffs

Narrator
We are going to tell you how one small incident led Martin Luther King to become President of an organization called The Montgomery Improvement Association (MIA), which led all black people in the town of Montgomery to boycott using the buses as a protest against discrimination.

The year was 1955 and the date of the incident was Thursday 1st December. To understand the significance of the incident, it is necessary to understand that in America (and elsewhere in the world, like South Africa until fairly recently), black people were being treated very unfairly and as second-class citizens. Black and white children could not go to the same schools, they could not eat together in the same restaurants, or travel together on the same bus. Black people could not vote, they often worked longer hours than white people and were paid far less.

Martin Luther King was a Baptist Minister who believed in non-violent action to achieve freedom from oppression and injustice. Rosa Parks was an ordinary black citizen in the town of Montgomery, Alabama.

Rosa Parks

I'm Rosa Parks and I'm the black lady who started the whole episode off. You see, I had been working very hard all day and I was tired and worn out and my feet were aching. I simply sat down in one of the front seats of this bus, which was reserved for white people only.

Bus driver

You can't sit there, you black woman. Just who do you think you are, giving yourself airs and graces? That seat is reserved for white people only. Get to the back of the bus at once.

Rosa Parks

(*Politely*) I'm very sorry, but I'm just too tired to move. I'm not doing any harm and I feel that I have as much right to this seat as anyone else. I pay the same bus fare as the white people, therefore I should be able to sit on the same seats. I'm not going to move.

Bus driver

Don't you answer me back. I shall call the Police Inspector and have you thrown off the bus, if you don't do as you are told at once. (*Rosa Parks remains sitting. Bus driver speaks into mobile phone.*) Right . . . Chief Inspector? Yes, would you come at once, I've got some black woman here who is refusing to sit on the seats reserved for blacks . . . yes, you will come at once! Right, well the bus won't move until you get here. (*Puts down the phone and waits a few seconds. Enter Chief of Police.*)

Chief of police

I am placing you under immediate arrest. I shall take you back to the Police Station with me, where you will be charged with this offence. I shall make sure that you are severely punished. Do you understand me? (*Rosa Parks is frog-marched off the stage.*)

Narrator

But Mrs Parks was a hard-working and highly respected black lady and news of her arrest soon spread throughout the Montgomery community. The Rev Ralph Abernathy, Rosa's own Church Minister, went to see Martin Luther King to persuade him to help organise a boycott of all buses because of this unfair treatment of Rosa.

Rev Ralph Abernathy

Look, Martin, we have just got to do something about Rosa's arrest. It's simply not right. She wasn't doing any harm. Isn't it time we stood up for ourselves and protested about the way black people are being treated?

Martin Luther King

Yes, but only if we can find a non-violent way of protesting. I am a Christian and I believe that we must do as Jesus taught us to do and that is to love our enemies and do good to those who hate us, even when they do terrible things to us.

Rev Ralph Abernathy

Well, we black people could refuse to use any of the city buses – and since we are the largest group of bus-users, the bus companies would soon lose so much money that they would have to listen to us.

Narrator

That night 40,000 leaflets were printed and distributed to all the black people's homes asking them to boycott the buses on Monday 5th December 1955. The leaflet asked the people to walk to work or to share cars or take taxis and then to come to a large meeting to be held at Martin Luther King's own Church that evening. Many people boycotted the buses that day and about 4,000 people turned up at the meeting. Martin Luther King was elected President of MIA.

(*Enter crowd of black people who sit down to listen to Martin Luther King.*)

The black people sat down and listened to what Martin Luther King had to say.

Martin Luther King

Thank you all for coming and thank you all for boycotting the buses today. We must keep up the boycott and encourage all our black brothers and sisters to participate in this non-violent action. We need you black taxi drivers to charge only the equivalent bus fare instead of your usual fare and we need people with their own cars to give lifts to those who cannot get to work. Many of you will have to walk to work, can you keep this up? 'We are doing this because we are tired of being segregated and humiliated, tired of being kicked about . . . we have no alternative but to make a protest. We have been amazingly patient. But we have come here tonight for freedom and justice.' (Source: N. Richardson, *Martin Luther King*, published by Hamish Hamilton, 1983.)

Narrator

The black people at the meeting all agreed to keep up the boycott of the buses until all people, black and white, were treated equally. Martin Luther King was threatened, his house was bombed and he was arrested on many false charges. The boycott proved highly successful, most black people refused to travel on the buses and so the bus companies began to lose vast sums of money.

Yet it took just over a year before the protest finally bore fruit and came to an end in December 1956. The Supreme Court in Washington declared that segregation on public transport was illegal and ordered the bus companies to end their discrimination. So Martin Luther King had won a major battle for black people in America, but this was only the beginning. There were many other battles to follow before his untimely death in March 1968 in Memphis, Tennessee, when Martin Luther King was shot dead by a white ex-convict.

Prayer

Holy God, help us to be brave and courageous and to speak out when we see any form of injustice or racial discrimination. May we never be the ones who discriminate against another person because of the colour of their skin, race or religion. Help us to be active in defending minority groups. Amen

Hymn

Sing one of the songs from the Civil Rights Movement, such as the Negro Spiritual 'We Shall Overcome' or 'Go Tell It On The Mountain'.

Poem

End the assembly by reading Martin Luther King's own words 'I Have a Dream'.

I Have a Dream

I have a dream that one day
every valley shall be exalted
every hill and mountain
shall be made low
the rough places will be made plain
and the crooked places
will be made straight
and the glory of the Lord
shall be revealed
and all flesh shall see it together.

This is our hope.
With this faith,
we will be able to hew out
of the mountains of despair
a stone of hope.

With this faith
we will be able to transform
the jingling discords of our nation
into a beautiful symphony
of brotherhood.

With this faith
we will be able to work together
to pray together
to struggle together
to go to jail together
knowing that we will be free one day.

Martin Luther King

Resources

Hunter, N., *Martin Luther King. Great Lives Series*, Wayland, 1985.*
A mixture of photographs and good illustrations, the book tells the main story of Martin's life and beliefs. It contains a useful document of important dates, glossary of words and terms and recommends books for further reading.

Hunter, N., *Twenty Campaigners For Change*, Wayland, 1987.*
Part of a series of books, i.e. 'Twenty Names in Medicine', 'Sport', 'Explorers', 'Tyrants', 'Classical Music', 'Inventors', etc. This book describes Martin Luther King and Bob Geldof amongst the twenty names. Suitable for 7–11 year olds.

Lynch, E., *The Life of Martin Luther King Jr*, Heinemann, 2005.
Actual photographs of Martin Luther King and his family are used in this excellent book. There is a map to show where he was born, where he went to college, and where Rosa Parks was arrested, etc. Books giving further information are recommended, and a web-site set up by Martin Luther King's wife displays their photographs about Martin's life. It is a very clear,

easy to read book, cataloguing his life and what he believed in. The web-site given is: www.thekingcentre.com

Lloyd Jones, R., *Martin Luther King*, Usborne Publishing Ltd, 2006.
An excellent book that uses contemporary photographs. The publisher also offers a web-site at www.usborne-quicklinks.com and then type in Martin Luther King, to hear some of Martin's famous speeches.

Malam, J., *Martin Luther King. Tell Me About Pioneers*, Evans Brothers Ltd, 1999.
Once again, good use is made of contemporary photographs.

Owen, R. J., *Free At Last: Martin Luther King*, RMEP, 1998.
This book is part of the excellent 'Faith in Action' Series which looks at other great lives, i.e. Cicely Saunders, Jackie Pullinger, Elizabeth Fry, Mahatma Gandhi, etc.

Peace Pledge Union, *Martin Luther King: An Interactive CD*, PPU, 2005.
The CD can be played on a CD player or a PC. It contains lesson plans and is available at a cost of £10 plus postage. Available from PPU, 1 Peace Passage, London N7 0BT. Tel: 020 7424 9444. Fax: 020 7482 6390. E-mail: info@ppu.org.uk

Rediger, P., *Civil Rights. Great African Americans*, Crabtree Publishing Co., 1996.
Contains a chapter on Rosa Parks, her life and protest. Suitable for 8 year olds and over.

Richardson, N., *Martin Luther King*, Hamish Hamilton, 1983.*
Part of the 'Profile' Series, suitable for 7–11 year olds.

Some books marked with an asterisk may now be out of print, but are still found in many school libraries.

William Wilberforce

The author was brought up in Africa and, as part of the school history curriculum was taught about the terrible slavery that had occurred in her part of the world some two hundred years earlier.

As children, we pored over the horrifying pictures of the slave ships, with all their human agony and suffering and we retraced the route the enforced slaves would have taken, by walking down the slave tunnels to where the waiting ships would have been moored to accept their human cargo. Deeply affected by our experiences, we thought that this should never be allowed to happen again.

That is why it seems utterly intolerable that slavery should still exist over much of the world today. Places like Kashmir and Morocco and many parts of India where children are enslaved in the carpet-making industry; Haiti, where Haitians are enslaved in the sugar-cane fields and the Gulf, where children are sold to work as camel jockeys, to name but a few areas in the world.

Anti-Slavery International does much to draw the world's attention to modern-day slavery and conditions of human misery. In their fight against this appalling trade, they have school resource lists, DVDs and video teaching packs, exhibitions, books, book lists, fact sheets, newsletters and posters, some free and some available at modest prices. Much of the material is relevant for upper primary and secondary schools, but teachers would need to use their own professional judgement as to the suitability of the materials for their particular class. See the web-site: www.antislavery.org for assembly ideas.

The opening of the International Slavery Museum in Liverpool in 2007 is another great resource for those who live near enough to visit, but it also has an excellent web-site: www.liverpoolmuseums.org.uk (address below).

The film *Amazing Grace* (PG) is suitable for the over eight year olds and perhaps could be enjoyed after the children have studied and researched William Wilberforce's life, the important dates of which are given below.

1   He was born on 24 August 1759 in Hull.
2   In 1776 he went to Cambridge University where he met William Pitt, who was later to become his friend and the Prime Minister of England.
3   In 1780 at the age of twenty-one, he was elected as a Member of Parliament; a post he was to hold for forty-five years until ill-health forced him to retire in 1825.
4   Early on in his career, he enjoyed an extravagant life-style and spent much of his time gambling and enjoying himself.
5   Whilst on a tour of Europe, he became converted to Christianity, which changed his whole attitude to life and his way of living.

6 In 1787 a group of opponents to the Slave Trade (including some eminent Quakers) asked Wilberforce to represent them in Parliament by fighting against the Slave Trade.

7 The following year Wilberforce suffered a serious illness, yet, again and again, he attempted to push a bill through Parliament to abolish the Slave Trade. Each time the bill was defeated in the House of Lords.

8 However, in 1807, Parliament finally agreed to abolish the Slave Trade, but people in the British Colonies were still allowed to own their slaves. So Wilberforce fought to abolish this practice too.

9 In 1825 Wilberforce had to retire from Parliament through ill-health.

10 In 1833, just a month before his death in July, the Slavery Abolition Act was finally passed.

You will need to find out from the web-sites below, where and what type of 'Child Labour'/ 'Forced Labour' still exists across the world today, before doing the following assembly.

For the assembly, it is suggested that a world map is pinned up for everyone to see and then after telling the children how slavery was abolished in this country by the actions of William Wilberforce and his associates, areas where slavery still exists today could be plotted on the map. Approximately ten children could be involved. Each child could carry a placard describing the type of child labour/forced labour that exists and then place a red marker on the area of the world where this type of slavery is being perpetrated. It is important for children to know that individual actions can change situations.

End the assembly with the 1948 Universal Declaration of Human Rights: Article 4, which says: 'No-one shall be held in slavery or servitude; slavery and the slave trade shall be prohibited in all their forms.'

Reflection

There should be a time of quiet reflection as the school and individuals contemplate their response to slavery in the world today. Can we do anything about it? Can we make a difference?

Hymn

Sing the Hymn 'Amazing Grace' in *Mission Praise* published by Marshall Pickering. This version was written by Dave Bilbrough/Thank You Music, but the original version was written by a reformed Sea Captain of a slave ship, John Newton.

Useful addresses

Anti-Slavery International
Thomas Clarkson House,
The Stableyard,
Broomgrove Road,
London SW9 9TL
Tel: 02075 018920
e-mail: antislavery@antislavery.org
web-site: www.antislavery.org

International Slavery Museum
Dock Traffic Office
Albert Dock
Liverpool L3 4AX
Tel: 01514 784499
web-site: www.liverpoolmuseums.org.uk

Part 5

Peaceful Places and Challenges

Take Time to be Still
Breathing Exercises

In our busy lives, we all need to learn to take time to be still, to find peace, to be at peace. This can be a very 'peaceful' assembly! Ask the children, sitting exactly where they are to take a deep breath, breathing in peace and blowing out all the things that are cluttering their minds, all the things that are worrying them, all their fears and anxieties. Repeat this breathing exercise several times, before reading the following poem:

Take Time

Take time to think;
It is the source of power.
Take time to read;
It is the beginning of wisdom.
Take time to play;
It is the secret of staying young.
Take time to be quiet;
It is the opportunity to seek God.
Take time to be aware;
It is the opportunity to help others.
Take time to love and be loved;
It is God's greatest gift.
Take time to laugh;
It is the music of the soul.
Take time to be friendly;
It is the road to happiness.
Take time to dream;
It is what the future is made of.
Take time to pray;
It is the greatest power on earth.

(Author unknown)

Perhaps each of the couplets could be painted by a group of children and displayed around the hall with the words underneath, to serve as a useful reminder about being at peace. Or some children could learn the poem and repeat it as a choral exercise, with different groups speaking the different parts.

Do the breathing exercises again and this time, end the assembly with a time of quiet reflection or private prayer, repeating the words, 'Take time to be quiet; it is the opportunity to seek God'.

To maintain the peaceful attitude, tell the children that there will be no hymns this morning and that they must creep back to their classrooms in silence!

A Monastery

How a Medieval Monk Used to Live

Preparation

Some preparation is needed for this project. Below are listed various aspects of monastic life for further research and for presentation to a school assembly in art, drama, written work, and scientific form.

Monastic life

The children can write about the Rules of St Benedict, who lived from 480–543 AD. See St Benedict (Trans by Doyle, L.J.), *Rule of St Benedict*, Liturgical Press, 1986. Briefly, days were divided into almost equal parts for worship; for private prayer or study; and for domestic or manual work. Obedience to the Abbot was very important.

The vows

A monk had to promise to give up the outside world and everything he owned and to obey the Monastic Rule and the Abbot.

A typical monastery

Research the following buildings and grounds:
1. Church, 2. Abbot's House, 3. Chapter House, 4. Dormitory, 5. Refectory, 6. Laver, 7. Kitchen, 8. Infirmary, 9. Guest House, 10. Malt House, 11. Cloister, 12. Tithe Barn, 13. Stables, 14. Gatehouse to Farmland, 15. Orchard, 16. Vegetable Garden.

Daily worship

Find out all you can about medieval music. There were a series of eight services called the Divine Office or Hours: Matins 12pm; Prime 6am; Terce 9am (these times changed according to the winter or summer); Sext 12am; None 3pm; Vespers 6pm; Compline 7pm.

High Mass took place at 10am. During the service, there were psalms, prayers and lessons. The singing was called the Gregorian chant. Very often the church was decorated with stained glass windows, carved screens and wall paintings.

Find examples of these and let the children draw and paint their own windows and wall paintings.

Discipline

Meetings took place in the Chapter House where the daily running of the community was discussed. Confession and correction also took place here. Punishment for wrong-doers generally meant eating bread and drinking water and sometimes it meant a beating.

Let the children write about punishments today. What is appropriate, what is not?

Studies

Holy studies took place in the Cloister. There was a time for study between the Chapter Meeting and High Mass; and again in the afternoons. Senior monks would work in the North walk; juniors worked in the Western walk; novices worked in the Eastern walk. Seniors would teach juniors about the Scriptures and monastic way of life.

Let the children make a ground floor plan of the Cloister (see below for an example), noting any special features.

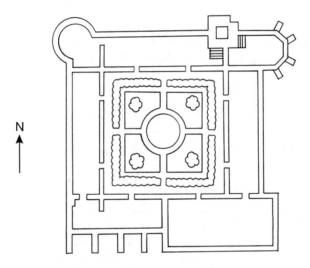

N

Food and drink

Monks ate in the Refectory or Frater. Usually only one meal a day was served, after High Mass; but sometimes during the summer another light meal was served again in the evening. Those monks who were ill were given an extra ration of bread soaked in beer. The meal usually consisted of beans or eggs or cheese and vegetables, usually served with bread and beer, wine or mead to drink; followed by fresh fruit. Fish was eaten on Fridays and chicken, pork and spicy cakes would be served on special occasions. One of the juniors would read during the meal and also take it in turns to serve the other monks. If a monk spilt any food, he had to do a penance. All the left-overs were given to the poor.

Discuss meals today; your favourite meals and likes and dislikes. Draw up comparative lists.

Recreation and work

The afternoon began with a period of rest and recreation. In summer this might take the form of a game of bowls in the garden. In winter, they might go to the Calefactory or warming room, or play games like chess in the Cloister. After None (3pm) most monks went to the Cloister to study. Others looked after the Monastery buildings and equipment like the cooking equipment. Monks would do such work as stone carving, wood carving and make stained glass windows.

Research other medieval games. Visit a Cathedral or Church and see beautiful carved wooden screens.

Books and the scriptorium

The scribes worked in the Scriptorium. Some composed, others specialised in illustration. Others spent time in copying manuscripts. Books were written on parchment with goose-quill pens. Initial letters were enlarged and decorated; borders were decorated. Paints were made out of natural substances and plants. Many were gilded with gold leaf. Books were bound in leather and precious stones, and were fastened with a clip.

Let the children experiment with natural paints and dyes. Try tie and dye or writing with a goose-quill pen. Let the children decorate the borders of their work and experiment with the initial letter of their own name.

Health care

Every twelve weeks, monks had to go to the infirmary or farmery for blood-letting, because they thought that it was beneficial to their health. This meant three days rest for the monk.

Toilets were called the *necessarium*; the washroom was called the *laver*. The *infirmarian* looked after sick patients using herbal medicine from plants grown in the *herbarium*.

Is there a herb garden near you? Can you list and identify some of the plants? What are they used for? For instance, mint was used for indigestion and to cure headaches. Other herbs included sage, rue, rosemary, thyme, cumin, etc. (see book list in the Resources section).

Pilgrims

The monks' basic rule was to treat all people 'as if they were Christ himself'. Beggars and lepers stayed in the Monastery's Charity House or Almonry. Most visitors were looked after by the *'Hospitarius'* or Guest Master. They were given food and shelter and would repay the Monastery by giving gifts of money.

Also, those fleeing from the law could be given 'sanctuary' in the Church. They were allowed to stay for forty days after confessing their crime to the Abbot. Then they had to go before a Magistrate, before going into exile.

Resources

Baker, M., *Discovering the Folklore of Plants*, Shire Publications Ltd., 1996.

Bown, D., *The RHS Encyclopaedia of Herbs and Their Uses*, Dorling Kindersley, 2003.

Boyd, A., *Life in a Medieval Monastery*, Cambridge University Press, 1991.

Bremness, L., *Pocket Encyclopaedia of Herbs*, Dorling Kindersley, 1999.

Caselli, G., *A Medieval Monk*, Macdonald, 1986.*

Crabtree Publishing, *Life in a Medieval Monastery*, Crabtree Publishing, 2004. (For juniors, the book describes why people entered a monastery, their vows and what they did day and night. The different customs of Roman Catholic, and Eastern Orthodox churches; a Buddhist Monk; schedules and rules of a Benedictine Monastery; Cistercians, Mendicant Friars and Dominican orders are all described.)

Chrisp, P., *The Medieval Church*, Wayland, 1996. (Wonderful photographs and illustrations, with a section on life in a Monastery for Monks and Nuns.)

Hill, T., *The Contemporary Encyclopaedia of Herbs and Spices*, Hungry Minds Inc., 2005.

Hunter, N., *A Medieval Monk*, Wayland, 1987.*

Knowles, D.D., *The Monastic Orders in England: A History of Their Development*, Cambridge University Press, 2004 (for teachers / advanced study).

Place, R., *Medieval Britain*, Wayland 1989* (for pupils).

St Benedict (trans by L.J. Doyle), *Rule of St Benedict*, Liturgical Press, 1986* (for teachers).

Sutton, H.T., *The Heritage Book of Cathedrals*, Heritage Books & Longman, 1985* (for pupils and teachers).

Unstead, R.J., *Monasteries*, A & C Black, 1979* (for pupils).

Waltz, N.D., *The Herbal Encyclopaedia: A Practical Guide to the Many Uses of Herbs*, iUniverse.com, 2004.

Wright, N., *Beautiful Cathedrals of Britain*, Marshall Cavendish, 1978.*

* Although these books are now out of print, they remain classic children's books on the subject and can be found in most libraries.

My Secret Place

The aim of engaging children in this piece of work is two-fold; first, it can be an exercise in descriptive writing; second, it can be a sharing of experience, reverence and awe in a school assembly.

In order to avoid writing that is just a list of descriptive words, the teacher can help to focus the children's perception in the following way:

1 First, encourage the children to describe their secret place using their *senses*. Sight and touch are obvious senses for inclusion in the work, but try and encourage the children to focus on sound, smell and possibly taste (i.e. if the secret place is in a garden, or the sound/smells on a farm).

2 Second, encourage the children to use their *imagination* – what do they think about or feel when they are in their secret place? What would they like to do – a flight of the imagination, wishful thinking, etc. A good story to promote this sort of discussion is Sendak's *Where the Wild Things Are* for the youngest children, when Max becomes King of the Wild Things and controls them. *The Secret Garden* is another good starting point/story for older children. Do the children sometimes meet another personality in their secret place (i.e. the Shepherd; or their Grandmother; or an imaginary person; or a pet)? Could they describe such an interaction? In this way, the teacher can really extend the children's imaginative work.

3 Finally, encourage the children to use their *reasoning skills* to explain why they chose a particular place. How did they find it, what are the benefits of having such a place?

For the Assembly, various children could:

1 *Read* their piece of work aloud to the rest of the school.

2 *Pray* – the children could draw the assembly together with short prayers thanking God for their ability to withdraw from the hustle and bustle of everyday living; for times to be quiet and to enjoy silence; for the ability to use their minds to think and to make plans; for a place to be perfectly at peace.

3 *Story* – this could be linked with Jesus' need to be quiet and to be alone before an important event. See the following Bible stories.

Bible references

Luke Chapter 2, verses 42–49: The child Jesus leaves his family and returns to the Temple to learn.

Luke Chapter 4, verses 1–14: Before Jesus begins his ministry, he goes alone to the desert and is tempted by the devil.

Luke Chapter 6, verse 12: Jesus needs to be alone to pray. He goes to the mountain and spends the whole night in prayer before choosing the twelve disciples.

Luke Chapter 9, verse 28: Jesus takes Peter, James and John into the quiet hills to pray. This is the place of the transfiguration.

Luke Chapter 21, verse 37: Jesus teaches in the Temple by day, but at night he goes to the quiet Mount of Olives.

Matthew Chapter 26, verses 36–50: Jesus withdraws to a quiet place to pray in the Garden of Gethsemane before his death.

There are many more references in the Bible.

Easter
The Paradise Garden

The aim of this assembly is to help children understand the Christian view of new life after death. Easter is an extremely difficult concept for young children to grasp and yet somehow, the meaning of what happened to Jesus on the cross, why he died and rose again, must be conveyed to the children; i.e. Jesus died for the love of mankind, sacrificing Himself for the sins of the world. Christians believe He rose again and receives those who believe in Him, into Paradise at the end of their lives.

The following story is an imaginary tale, in which the small boy represents Jesus. The man with his hands and feet pierced by nails also represents Jesus, the grown man, who is crucified, dies on the cross and rises again. He returns to take those who believe in Him back into Paradise to live with Him for ever.

By implication, this story also indicates that people change as a result of meeting Jesus. For instance, the Giant is very sorry for being selfish and tries to make amends. Then, at the end of his life, Jesus receives him into Paradise to live with Him.

The children could mime the story as the Narrator reads it.

You will need the following

Characters	Props and costumes
Flowers	Flower head-dresses
Trees	Sandwich boards showing green trees on one side/bare silver trees on the other side
Birds	Bird masks
Children playing	Skipping ropes, balls, etc.
Giant	Large collar, big boots
Jack Frost	Silver clothes/silver wand
Snow	White tunic/tights
North Wind	Blue tunic/tights
Hail	Black tunic + tambourine
Jesus as a boy	Simple tunic
Jesus as a man	Simple tunic
	Notice 'Trespassers will be Prosecuted'

Once upon a time a long time ago, a huge Giant lived in a massive castle, which was surrounded by the most beautiful garden you have ever seen.

(Enter flowers, trees and birds who take up their positions and freeze)

The Giant had been away from his castle and garden for about seven years while he visited his friends in another country. While he was away, the children living near the castle used to play in his garden.

(Enter group of children playing games such as hopscotch, skipping, football)

But one day the Giant returned *(Enter Giant)* and he was so angry to find the children playing in his beautiful garden that he stamped and shouted, shook his fists at them and shooed them all out. Then he built a huge wall around the garden and hammered into the ground, a large notice that read 'TRESPASSERS WILL BE PROSECUTED'. The poor children now had nowhere to play, so they played in the road, which was very dangerous indeed.

(These actions are mimed by the Giant; the children sadly leave the garden)

Then the flowers in the garden began to wither and die. *(Flowers mime the action)* Outside the garden it was Spring, but inside the garden it remained bleak Winter. First Jack Frost came and he painted all the trees silver and they lost their leaves. *(Jack Frost enters and as he touches each tree with his wand, they slowly turn around to show their silver, leafless side)*

Then Snow came and spread a white blanket over all the plants and trees. *(Snow mimes the action)*

Then North Wind blew a gale over the garden and sent all the little birds scurrying away to find shelter. *(The birds hurry away)*

Finally, Hail arrived and rattled on the roof tops and beat on the windows and clattered on the grass. *(Hail beats on his tambourine as he dances all over the floor)*

The Giant began to get very worried when he saw his miserable garden – no Spring, and perhaps no Summer and no Autumn. Then one day, the Giant heard a linnet singing. It was the most beautiful sound he had heard for a very long time. He looked out of the window and saw the trees had turned green, flowers were blooming and the birds were flying around happily. Spring had strangely returned after all.

(Each group mimes the action in turn, as their part is read out)

Spring had returned because the children had found a small hole in the wall and had crept through to play in the garden once again. *(Children enter.)* However, in one corner of the garden, it was still Winter and underneath a huge oak tree, stood a small boy crying. He was crying because he could not climb the tree, like all the other children. *(The action is mimed)*

Suddenly, the Giant realised how selfish he had been. He rushed outside and lifted the young boy into the tree. The other children ran away because they were afraid of the Giant. *(The action is mimed)* But the little boy threw his arms around the Giant's neck and kissed him. The Giant decided to encourage all the other children to return to his garden. He knocked down the wall and ripped up the 'Trespassers' notice. Gradually, the children came to play every day, but the young boy was never seen again and this made the Giant sad, as he loved him most of all.

Many years went by and different children played in the garden. The Giant grew old and more and more tired. *(All these actions are mimed)*

One day in the middle of Winter, the Giant looked out of his window and saw that the large oak tree at the bottom of his garden had turned a brilliant gold. Underneath the tree stood the boy, now grown into a man. The Giant rushed to meet him but stopped in horror when he saw the young man's hands and feet had been pierced by nails. The Giant was terribly upset and asked the young man who had done this awful thing to him. The man replied that these were the wounds of Love and that his hands had been pierced for all the wrong-doing in the world. As the Giant had been kind and let him and all the other children play in his garden, now he would take the Giant back to his own garden, called Paradise.

When the little children came to play the next day, they found the Giant underneath the huge oak tree, where he had died peacefully, knowing that today he would be with his friend in Paradise.

'The Paradise Garden' by Elizabeth Peirce is an adaptation of *The Selfish Giant* by Oscar Wilde.

The teacher needs to draw the threads together and explain that when people meet Jesus, they try and change their behaviour, like the Giant. Jesus died on a cross as a sacrifice for all the wrong things in the world. He rose again and takes those who believe in Him to live with Him in Paradise at the end of their lives.

Hymn

No. 130, 'All in an Easter Garden' in *Come and Praise 2*, published by the BBC.

All in an Easter Garden

1. All in an Eas - ter gar - den Be - fore the break of

day, An an - gel came for Je - sus, And rolled the stone a -

way. And when his friends came seek - ing, With myrrh and spi - ces

rare, They found the an - gels at the door, But Je - sus was not there.

1. All in an Easter garden,
   Before the break of day,
   An angel came for Jesus,
   And rolled the stone away.
   And when his friends came seeking,
   With myrrh and spices rare,
   They found the angels at the door,
   But Jesus was not there.

2. All in an Easter garden,
   Where water lilies bloom,
   The angels gave their message,
   Beside an empty tomb;
   'He is not here, but come and see
   The place where Jesus lay:
   The Lord of life is risen indeed,
   For this is Easter Day.'

Prayer

Father God, we thank you for sending your Son Jesus, who died and rose again, giving us hope for a new life to come in a paradise garden. Amen

Reflection

Think about love; when someone encounters love as the Giant did in the story, the result is that they change for the better. To whom could you show love today?

Development for older children

Read the account of the Crucifixion and Resurrection in Luke Chapters 23 and 24. Find out about other Spring Festivals, such as Purim and Pesach (Judaism), Baisakhi and Hola Mohalla (Sikhism).

Poetry

Read the poems below entitled 'Easter' or 'Thirty Pieces of Silver' by Elizabeth Peirce.

Easter

May something of your resurrection joy,
spill out into our lives today.
May something of your resurrection peace,
break through the walls with which we surround ourselves.

May something of your resurrection forgiveness,
help us to bring forgiveness to others.
For it is in doing this, that we shall make our world a better place to live in.

It is in understanding that death is not the end,
that will give us the freedom to live today to the full.
It is in knowing that you died for others,
that will transform how we treat one another now.

Elizabeth Peirce

Thirty Pieces of Silver

Sold for thirty pieces of silver
Betrayed by a kiss.
Denied by his friends
Who was this?

Nailed to a cross
And buried in a tomb
Was this the Son of God?
If not, whom?

Three days later,
The stone rolled away.
Only clothing left
Exactly as he lay.

Mary wept in the garden, until she saw
Jesus, whom she had been looking for.
I am alive, do not weep,
Joyfully she fell at her master's feet.

Elizabeth Peirce

Guru Nanak's Needle
A Sikh Tale

This lovely Sikh story is very similar in style and content to the parable Jesus told about it being 'harder for a rich man to enter the Kingdom of Heaven, than it would be for a camel to pass through the eye of a needle'. The main point being, that both Guru Nanak and Jesus were saying the same thing, not to build up riches on earth that could be given to the poor, the hungry and the needy now.

Once upon a time, there lived a kindly Sikh man who was very rich indeed. He wore the finest clothes, had hundreds of servants and gave the most lavish feasts for all his friends. The food *left over* would have kept many poor families in meals for a month or more.

One day, the rich man decided to give a very special feast for Guru Nanak. To his utter delight, the Guru accepted his kind invitation. Large bowls of food were bought and prepared and the feast was so grand that even his guests gasped when they saw all the sumptuous dishes set before them. Looking all around, the rich man was very pleased indeed with himself and all that he had provided, his lavish meal and all his finery.

Guru Nanak duly arrived and was seated in the place of honour next to the rich man. As the guests helped themselves to the luscious food, the rich man asked Guru Nanak if there was anything *more* he needed to do before he went to Heaven.

Guru Nanak was very thoughtful for a moment and then, very carefully, he unpinned a needle that was in his clothes and gave it to the rich man saying, 'I want you to take very great care of this needle for me, for the rest of your life and when it is time for you to die, I want you to return it to me in Heaven.'

The rich man thanked Guru Nanak very much indeed for trusting him with this special needle. He felt greatly honoured to have been chosen to do this small thing for his beloved Guru. Proudly, he went away and told his wife what Guru Nanak had asked him to do. He showed her the needle that had been entrusted to his care.

But instead of being as proud and as honoured as he was, his wife laughed loudly at him and said, 'When you die, how do you think you are going to give the needle back to Guru Nanak? You can take nothing with you, you know.'

Suddenly, realising that this was true, the rich man saw his awful mistake. Of course, he could not give the needle back to Guru Nanak in Heaven. Sadly, he returned to his Guru for an explanation. Very gently, Guru Nanak told the rich man that if he could not take a needle with him to Heaven, how could he take all his money and riches with him to Heaven?

So at last, the rich man knew and understood what he must do. He decided to learn from his Guru's teaching. He gave away all his money to all the poor people who needed it. He gave food to the hungry and starving, and he helped anyone who came to him in adversity and supplied whatever was necessary.

In this way, he took the love, gratitude and many blessings from all the people whom he had helped, with him to Heaven when he died, because no-one can take away all this kindness and goodness.

Helping others in the Sikh faith is very important indeed. It is called 'sewa' or service.
(This story has been adapted from A. Ganeri, *Sikh Stories*, Evans Bros Ltd., 2007)

Reflection

Give the children time to think about this lovely story and to make a mental list of how they could serve others today. Perhaps the children could make a class book later, with all their ideas and pictures of what they could do.

Prayer

This is an extract from 'The Sukhmani' (The Psalm of Peace), probably written before 1604. It is not part of the regular Sikh prayers, but it is often read for guidance and inspiration. The text is slightly adapted from M. A. Macauliffe's *The Sikh Religion*, S. Chand & Co., Delhi, 1963.

> On the way where the miles cannot be counted,
> The name of God shall be thy (your) provision;
> On the way where there is pitch darkness,
> The name of God shall accompany and light thee (you);
> On the way where nobody knows thee (you),
> The name of God shall be there to recognise thee (you).

Song: No. 6, 'Come to the Party', in *Game-Songs with Prof Dogg's Troupe*, published by A & C Black.

Poem

Now read the poem 'Waiting'.

> *Waiting*
>
> Waiting, waiting, waiting
> For the party to begin;
> Waiting, waiting, waiting
> For the laughter and din;
> Waiting, waiting, waiting
> With hair just so
> And clothes trim and tidy
> From top-knot to toe.
> The floor is all shiny,
> The lights are ablaze;
> There are sweetmeats in plenty
> And cakes beyond praise.
> Oh the games and dancing,
> The tricks and the toys,

The music and the madness
The colour and noise!
Waiting, waiting, waiting
For the first knock on the door –
Was ever such waiting,
Such waiting before?

© James Reeves from *Complete Poems for Children*
(Heinemann), reprinted by permission of the James Reeves Estate.

Resources

Ganeri, A., *Sikh Stories*, Evans Bros Ltd., 2007.
   This excellent book contains many other stories that are suitable for school assemblies.

Penney, S., *Sikhism: Introducing Religion Series*, Heinemann, 2006.
   Very well written, clearly set out, uses real photos and is packed with user-friendly material.
   Suitable for 5–11 year olds. Younger children could appreciate the pictures, older children
   would understand the more in-depth information that is given.

Peace Lies Within Myself

Peace of mind has little to do with being in a peaceful place. Children and adults have to learn peaceful strategies if they are to be at peace. One can be at peace in the noisiest, crowded place, or be in a turmoil in a quiet setting.

Read the following quotation, Philippians Chapter 4, verses 8–9:

> 'Finally, brethren, whatever is true, whatever is honourable, whatever is just, whatever is pure, whatever is lovely, whatever is gracious, if there is any excellence, if there is anything worthy of praise, think about these things. What you have learned and received and heard and seen in me, do; and the God of peace will be with you.'
>
> *(The quotation is from the Revised Standard Version of the Bible, copyright © 1946, 1952 and 1971 by the National Council of the Churches of Christ in the USA. Used by permission. All rights reserved.)*

Of course, being in a beautiful garden or peaceful place can aid peace of mind, but children and adults need to consciously list all those things that make for peace. So have an overhead projector or a flip-chart ready and ask the children to list some peaceful strategies. For example:

1 Thinking about lovely, beautiful, honourable things.
2 Flushing out of the mind any harmful, upsetting thoughts.
3 If one has done wrong, asking forgiveness from God and from one another.
4 Loving the unlovely. (A lovely story for this is *Shrek*: see details below.)
5 Giving one's time or talents for the good of others.
6 Forgetting about things that irritate and concentrating on things that enhance or enrich life.
7 Participating in joyful activities such as singing, laughing, games, or having fun.
8 Seeing people's good points and not dwelling on the bad.
9 Co-operation rather than conflict.
10 Respect for all people and for all living creatures.

End the assembly either with the story of *Shrek* or the picture book story *I Know Something You Don't Know* by Maria Enrica Agostinelli published by Ernest Benn Ltd. The picture book turns something one expects to be nasty into something that is lovely. For example, the last picture shows a rough looking tramp holding something behind his back on one side of the page, but when the page is turned, he is revealed holding a beautiful flower and the refrain is repeated 'But I know something you don't know'. Or one can tell the following story about the woman who always wanted to change people.

> A very devout lady went about the community always trying to reform people's bad habits. 'You shouldn't do this, you mustn't do that, you ought to do so and so.' The people she met all looked frightened and always tried to avoid her in case something that they were doing met with her disapproval, as they could never meet her rigid, high standards. Then one day, she heard a minister in a church say that in Jesus' eyes, the people with faults were the very people that he loved. So she tried to look at people through Jesus' eyes. She tried to love them rather than trying to change them and she suddenly discovered that they were already lovely and that it was not they who needed to change but herself. Jesus changes people from within; no amount of badgering people from without changes them. In loving others, she herself had been changed to see only their good points.

Prayer

Lord Jesus, give me peace within myself. Help me to love others as you do, to see only their good points. Help me to forget about those things that irritate me and to concentrate on those things that bring love, joy and peace to my community. Amen

Reflection

Reflect on being loving today. To whom can we show love today? How can we dispel gloom and doom and bring joy to others? Consider how to be at peace oneself, so that one can bring peace to others.

Hymn

No. 143, 'I've Got Peace Like a River' in *Come and Praise 2*, BBC.

Books

Agostinelli, M. E., *I Know Something You Don't Know*, Franklin Watts, 1970.
  You cannot always judge by outward appearances. Things turn out to be different from what they seem on the surface.
Steig, W. *Shrek*, Viking Kestrel Picture Books, 2006.
  An ugly hero marries an ugly princess and finds peace and happiness! Also available on video and DVD.

Putting Others Before Ourselves

An Islamic Tale

(It should be noted that when speaking Muhammad's name, Muslims pay respect to him, by saying the words 'Peace be upon him' or writing the sign for this,.)

The Prophet Muhammad taught that it was very important to put others before oneself. And true followers of Islam not only do this, but they teach their children to do so too. Therefore, it is very important that we dispel all the negative myths about Muslims that have been built up in the media and recent events and teach all our children that Muslims are very kind and generous and self-sacrificing.

The following story is a lovely traditional tale that emphasises this very point and can be read, just as it is (bearing in mind the point mentioned above), in a school assembly.

One day, when Muhammad (Peace be upon him) was teaching a group of his devout followers, a very poor man came to the door and asked for food, as he had not eaten for many days. Now it is very important for Muslims to share what they have with the poor, indeed it is part of their duty to give alms to the poor and to give away at least 2½ per cent of their savings. This is called *Zakat* and is one of the Pillars of Islam.

Muhammad had not eaten much himself that day and neither had many of his followers either, as times were very hard. But Muhammad looked around the group and asked 'Who will take this poor man home with him tonight and give him food to eat?'

Knowing that they all had very little to eat, there was complete silence at first. And then one brave man called Abdullah, spoke up. 'I will take this man home with me, O Prophet', he said, 'and share my food with him.'

So when the meeting had finished, Abdullah led the poor man down the street to his own house and opened the door. Abdullah's wife came to the entrance to greet him and Abdullah explained that he had brought an extra guest home for dinner.

Abdullah's wife welcomed her husband and the poor man into the house, then drew her husband aside saying, 'Could I have a brief word with you, dear husband, before dinner?' Seeing the worried look on his wife's face, he followed her out of the hearing of the very poor man.

Quickly, Abdullah's wife explained that she was just about to give all their meagre food rations to their three children and there certainly was not enough food left for the two grown-ups, let alone a third person.

Abdullah quickly devised a plan. He told his wife to send their children to bed without any food and he told her to whisper to them that this man's needs were greater than theirs. In addition, as there was so little food to go around, he and his wife would not eat anything at all, but give it all to their guest.

The children silently went to bed without a word, and Abdullah's wife continued to prepare the food. When she returned with it, the three adults sat down together and made ready to eat the meal.

Abdullah's wife suddenly said, 'I think there is too much light in here, I am going to turn down the lamp.' She turned the lamp down so low that they could hardly see each other, let alone see their plates. But cheerfully in the semi-darkness, she served all the food onto their guest's plate. Then she pretended to put much food onto her husband's plate and then pretended to put food onto her own plate.

Finally, she said, 'Right, let us eat our meal.' The very poor man tucked into his food and said, 'This is the finest food that I have ever tasted. Thank you so much for sharing your meal with me.' In the darkness, Abdullah and his wife pretended they were enjoying it too. They made much of putting something into their mouths, which was really nothing at all, so as not to embarrass their guest by letting him know that really they had nothing to eat.

When the poor man had finished his dinner, he left the house, thanking his hosts profusely for their kindness and generosity. He explained that he had not eaten for many days, but now he felt full and revived.

The next day, Abdullah went to see the Prophet Muhammad and before he managed to say a word, Muhammad somehow knew that Abdullah had sacrificed his own, his wife's and his children's needs, in order to feed a complete stranger. He told Abdullah that God would reward him greatly for what he had done.

Reflection

Ask the children how they think they would have felt about being sent to bed without any supper. Discuss whether they think that they could be that generous to a complete stranger. We may not be called upon to give away our food, but what other acts of kindness could we do? In what other situations could we put others first, before ourselves? Ask the children if they could put another person first today, in just one small way.

Resources

Aggarwal, M., *I Am A Muslim*, Franklin Watts, 1993.
  Lovely photographs of everyday life and worship.

Blount, K. (ed.), *Islam Eye-Witness Guides*, Dorling Kindersley, 2003.
  The usual very high standards of information and illustrations. 'Allah is the Light of the Heavens and the earth; the likeness of His Light is as a niche wherein is a lamp'.

Brine, A., *Religions Through Festivals: Islam*, Longman, 1994.
  Each section has key words and a very useful glossary at the back that gives an explanation. All the major festivals are included.

El-Droubie, Riadh, *My Muslim Life* Everyday Religion Series, Hodder Wayland, 2006.
  Uses lovely, contemporary photographs to show prayers, Makkah, a mosque, sharing a meal, best clothes for Id Celebrations, Id cards, etc. Suitable for 5–11 year olds.

Ganeri, A., *Islamic Stories*, Evans Bros Ltd., 2001.
  Includes the birth of the Prophet Muhammad; the story of Ibrahim and Ishmail; the story of Hajar (Hagar); the Prophet escapes to Medinah (Peace be upon them).

Ganeri, A., *Sacred Texts. The Qur'an and Islam*, Evans Bros Ltd., 2003.
  Tells the story of the Qur'an and how it came to be written down. 'And do good; indeed Allah loves the doers of good', Surah 2: 195.

Ganeri, A., *The Hajj Story*, Evans Bros Ltd., 2005.
    Wonderful illustrations. It describes Hajj; other stories include the story of Hajar (Hagar); the Prophet Ibrahim's wife; the story of Ibrahim and Ismail; Id-ul-Adha, at the end of Hajj when the story of Ibrahim and Ishmail is remembered and a sheep is sacrificed and given to the poor (Peace be upon them).

Hegedus, Umar, *Muslim Mosque, Keystones*, A & C Black, 2001.
    Intended for learning about citizenship in primary schools. Lovely photographs. Celebrates all the Muslim achievements like the astrolabe, etc. 'As-Salamu alaykum' means 'Peace be with you'.

Hirst, M., *Id-ul-Fitr*, Hodder Wayland, 2002.
    Excellent photographs.

Khan, Akbar Dad, *Muslim Imam*, Franklin Watts, 2001.
    Positive photographic images of the Imam's life and work and meetings with Church leaders.

Khan, Saniyasnain, *I'm Learning About the Prophet Muhammad*, Goodword Books, 2003.
    Lovely illustrations about the life of the Prophet (Peace be upon him).

Khan, S., *A Visit to Medinah. Qur'an Stories for Little Hearts*, Goodword Books, 2003.
    Tells the story of Muhammad's early life.

Khan, S., *Ramadan and the Qur'an*, Goodword Books, 2004.
    Lovely bright illustrations, suitable for the 5–11 age range, are a feature of all the books in this series. Teaches about Ramadan: Surah al-Baqarah 2: 183–185 and Surah al-Alaq 96: 1–5.

Khan, S., *The Ark of Nuh (Noah)*, Goodword Books, 2002.

Khan, S., *The Builder of the Kabah*, Goodword Books, 2002.
    Surah al-Baqarah 2: 125–127 and Surah al-Imran 3: 96–97.

Khan, S., *The First Man*, Goodword Books, 2001.
    Tells the story of Adam and Eve. In the Qur'an, Surah al-Imran 2: 30–38; Surah al-Maidah 5: 27–32; Surah al-Araf 7: 11–27; Surah Talta 20: 115–123; Surah Sad 38: 71–85 (Peace be upon them).

Khan, S., *The Iron Wall*, Goodword Books, 2003.
    About a King whose name was Dhul Qarnayan. In the Qur'an, Surah al-Kahf 18: 83–98.

Khan, S., *The Old Man's Prayer*, Goodword Books, 2004.
    Story of Zakariyya (Zechariah) and his son Yahya (John), Surah Maryam 19: 2–15 (Peace be upon them).

Khan, S., *The Story of Two Gardens*, Goodword Books, 2004.
    A nice story about a rich man and a poor man and their gardens. The poor man teaches the rich man to give the credit to Allah. Surah al-Kahf 18: 32–42.

Khan, S., *The Travels of the Prophet Ibrahim*, Goodword Books, 2001.
    Surah Ibrahim 14: 36–41; Surah al-Ankabut 29: 26–27.

Khattab, H., *Stories from the Muslim World*, Ta-Ha Publishers, 1996.
    An excellent book of stories about kindness and generosity. From the beginnings of Islam like the Prophet's childhood, to historical Muslim stories and famous Muslim tales. Particularly liked are 'The Two Brothers' and their generosity to each other, and 'A Dinner of Smells', etc. Includes background notes to the stories at the back of the book.

Knight, Khadijah, *My Muslim Faith* Rainbow Series, Evans Bros Ltd., 2006.
    There are six titles in this 'Rainbow' series introducing the reader to six of the main world religions. Lovely photographs to explain a child's faith. 'Allah teaches us to look after what He made and to live in peace.' Positive, helpful statements.

Marchant, K., *Muslim Festivals*, Hodder Wayland, 2000.
    Stories, a poem, a play and song are all in this excellent book. At the back, there is very useful

Festival information and a useful glossary. I particularly liked the story of 'Ali's Hajj', about a young man called Ali who gives his Hajj money to the Doctor for his sick friend and misses the actual pilgrimage. But his friends see him making the pilgrimage and conclude that it was through his generosity that his spirit was there and was affirmed by God as Ali's Hajj.

Penney, S., *Islam*, Heinemann, 2006.
   Includes a calendar of events, glossary and resources for further research. Also covers the main beliefs, festivals, worship, etc.

Senker, C., *I Am a Muslim*, Franklin Watts, 2005.
   Another excellent book about a child's life, in photographs.

Senker, C., *My Muslim Year* (A Year of Religious Festival Series), Hodder Children's Books, 2004.
   Contains a very useful Festival Calendar and glossary. All the major festivals are described.

Tames, R., *World Religions: Islam*, Franklin Watts, 2005.
   An excellent book showing the life, teaching and customs of Islam through photographs.

Taylor, K., *My Muslim Community*, Franklin Watts, 2005.
   Life and work in the community in Nottingham. Excellent photographs of hobbies, friends, food, school, clothes, prayer and celebrations.

The Warwick RE Project, 'Something To Share', *Muslim* (Bridges to Religions Series), Heinemann, 1994.
   Lovely contemporary photographs of a little Muslim girl and what she does at school, on her birthday, studies in the Qur'an, etc.

Wallace, H., *This is My Faith: Islam*, ticktock, 2006.
   Excellent photographs and useful glossary.

Wood, A., *Being A Muslim*, Batsford, 1986.
   Still found in libraries because it is an excellent resource.

Wood, J., *Muslim* Our Culture Series, Franklin Watts, 2003.
   Clear text for the 6–7 year old reader. Describes lives and culture through photographs.

Part 6

Assembly Plays to Promote Peace

It's Mine!

Start by asking the children what they understand by the word Peace. Get lots of ideas, accept opposites, i.e. Peace is quiet, it is restful, it is joyful, it means love, giving, sharing, etc. Opposites to Peace are: noise, fighting, wars, quarrelling, envy, greed, jealousy, disasters.

Then ask the children what to do when two sides cannot agree, what do you think they need? A peace-maker, a negotiator, a mediator.

Act the following sketch. It is intended for very young children.

You will need the following props and characters

A table and two chairs
Two children arguing over a toy
A peace-maker

First child: Give it to me.
Second child: No, it's mine.
First child: It's not yours, it belongs to the school.
Second child: I don't care, I've got it now, so it's mine.
First child: I want it.
Second child: You can't have it.
First child: I'll hit you, if you don't give it to me.
Peace-maker: Hey, hey, hey, you can't do that, that is how wars start; each person demanding to have their own way. Now let's start again, before war breaks out. What do you think they could do?

(Invite a little audience participation at this stage. What suggestions will the assembled children make? For example, the children can share, they can take it in turns, they can get another car, play co-operatively, etc.)

Now let's do the same sketch again, but this time, let's see if peace can dominate the situation.

First child: I want the car.
Second child: If you wait a minute, you can have a turn when I have finished playing with it.

First child: But I want it now.
Second child: Look here's another car you can play with until I have finished playing with this one. Then we can swap and take it in turns with this car.
First child: O.K. What shall we play?
Second child: Let's race the cars along this track.
First child: Is it my turn to play with the best car now?
Second child: In a minute, oh, alright, here you are.

The teacher needs to explain that all conflict is not always resolved so easily, but that the children must try to keep 'Peace' in their minds and whenever they are tempted to fight, they must try and find a better way. Seek the help of a peace-maker or teacher, so that disputes do not get out of control.

Prayer

Father God, help us not to fight each other. Help us to be ready to share and to take turns. Help us to see each other's point of view, instead of only wanting our own way all the time. We know, ultimately, that this leads to a more peaceful, loving place in which to live and work. Amen.

Hymn

No. 184, 'Peace Perfect Peace' in *Mission Praise* published by Marshall Pickering.

Poetry

Read the poem entitled 'Friendship' by Elizabeth Peirce.

Friendship

It suddenly occurred to me
That friendship is costly.
Making the first move
carries a risk. Fear of being
rejected, rebuffed, disregarded.
But how often do I
speak first, put out my hand, take time,
smile, move towards another person?
Not very often.
I wait in the hope that someone
will notice me, speak to me,
say I look nice,
invite me to tea.
How often do I see
that lonely person,
longing to be,
a part of me,
or me a part of him or her?
This humanity is our legacy.
And yet I fear,
Because it is costly.

Elizabeth Peirce

Strike Action

This sketch is for older children, but it is based on the same principles as 'It's Mine' on pp. 97–98. The teacher needs to explain that adults also have to learn to negotiate a peaceful settlement.

You will need the following characters

Two disputing sides, e.g. Management versus Workers'
Mediator

You will need the following props

Placards with: More Money
Longer Tea Breaks
Shorter Working Weeks
Better Conditions
Longer Holidays
Clipboards and mobile phones for Managers
Aprons and chefs' hats (or different trade) for Workers

The scene begins with the children all shouting the message on their placard, in turn, e.g. 'More Money', 'Longer Tea Breaks', 'Better Conditions', 'Longer Holidays'. Then they all stand at the back and freeze. It is then the turn of the Management (*with their clipboards and mobile phones*). In turn, they shout their answers back to the workers:

'We can't afford to pay you more money.'
'If you have longer tea breaks, the work won't get finished.'
'We cannot have a shorter week and pay you people to sit at home, we would go bankrupt.'
'We can't do it.'
'We won't do it.'
'Sack the lot of them.'

Mediator: When a dispute happens like this in industry, it is my job to call both sides together. We sit around a table and we discuss demands and possible solutions.

(*Both sides sit down on opposite sides of the table. The mediator sits at one end, facing the assembled school.*)

Mediator: Now, one at a time. (*To the workers*) What do you want?

First Worker: We want more money, I have a husband and baby at home and I have to pay the rent and all the food bills. This firm isn't paying me enough money. We want money and we want it now.

First Manager: We can't afford to pay you any more. If you don't produce the goods, we have got nothing to sell, so we cannot pay you for your work.

Mediator: How about, if you pay them a little more and they promise to keep up the production of goods?

Second Manager: Well, how much will they accept as a pay rise?

Second Worker: We are not asking for a fortune, we just want a fair deal.

Mediator: After many hours of talks, with a little give and take on both sides, the two sides agree and shake hands on the deal. (*The action is mimed.*)

The teacher needs to draw the whole thing together by saying something like, if you have a grievance, then you should discuss it openly and see if you can find a friendly solution. Sometimes, the solution will not be the one you want, but in learning to listen to one another, you may have to accept a compromise for the sake of peace.

Reflection

Think about how you could be more understanding in different situations throughout the day. Try to look at any disagreements from both sides. Listen to the other person more, instead of doing things your own way. What is it like to be in their shoes?

Prayer

Almighty God, it is not easy to keep the peace. I know it starts with me and how I treat my brothers and sisters, friends and neighbours. Help me to remember to seek the peaceful solution, so that in my small way, I can bring peace to others.

Hymn

No. 45, 'Father I Place into Your Hands The Things I Cannot Do', in *Mission Praise* published by Marshall, Morgan & Scott.

Pure Gold

A story to demonstrate that the ordinary things of life may turn out to be pure gold.

You will need the following characters

A ferry-boat man / woman
A passenger
A narrator
Two children (or more) wafting blue material to represent the waves

You will need the following props

A cardboard boat
Two oars
Strips of blue material to represent the waves
Bundle on a stick
Gold glitter

Narrator
We are going to show you, that sometimes, the things that we throw away, or think are unimportant, turn out to be very precious indeed.

This is the story of a passenger who needed to cross a river. The only way to cross the water was by a small ferry-boat. The ferry-boat man was tired, he had been ferrying people across the river all day long; backwards and forwards; backwards and forwards. It was getting late and nearly dark, and the ferry-boat man was about to pack up for the night, when the last passenger begged him to be taken across the water.

(The ferry-boat man with cardboard boat and oars is already in position. The children acting as the waves can begin to gently waft their material up and down. The passenger, with a bundle over one shoulder, enters.)

Passenger
Please sir, will you take me across the water? I know it's late, but I have been travelling all day and I must reach the other side before dark in order to continue my journey.

Ferry-boat man
It's too late. You should have come earlier. I've been taking people across the river all day and now I'm tired. I want to go home.

Passenger
Oh please sir, do take me, I will pay you well.

Ferry-boat man
How can you pay me well, you look like a poor man to me.

Passenger
Oh take me across, please.

Narrator
Grumbling, huffing and puffing, the ferry-boat man finally agreed to row the passenger across. (*The action is mimed.*) When they reached the other side, it was completely dark. The passenger stepped out of the boat, dug deep into his pockets and drew out what looked like wood shavings, to pay the ferry-boat man. The ferry-boat man was so disgusted that he threw the shavings into the water and shouted after the disappearing passenger. (*The action is mimed. The ferry-boat man can shout a few apt grumbles.*) The ferry-boat man then put the 'shavings' that had stuck to his hand into his pocket and started the long journey back across the river. (*The action is mimed.*)

In the morning the ferry-boat man felt in his pockets and pulled out the shavings that the passenger had given him the night before. To his horror, he stared at the shavings in his hand. They were not made of wood at all. They were shavings of pure gold, he had thrown them all away. He had thrown away a fortune because he had not looked carefully enough. (*A dramatic movement can be made, by throwing Christmas glitter dust into the air.*)

Sometimes, we are as silly as that ferry-boat man. We don't look carefully enough at the ordinary things in life. The beauty of a spider's web, a lovely sunset, or a tiny ladybird. We throw away moments of pure gold because we fail to treasure the occasion.

Sometimes we throw away friendships of pure gold, because we are not careful enough. We say something silly or unkind or hurtful. We forget to look and see how valuable that friend really is.

Prayer

Heavenly Father, help us today, to value carefully all things that come our way, as if they were objects of pure gold. Help us to value the ordinary things in life. Help us to value our friends and families. May we let others know, that we think they are pure gold. Amen.

Reflection

Think about those 'ordinary' things that are really very 'special' to you.

Hymn

No. 18, 'He Gave Me Eyes So I Could See' in *Come and Praise*, BBC.

Poetry

Read 'The Seed Shop' by Muriel Stuart in *Poems I Remember* published by Michael Joseph Ltd., London, 1960. Used with kind permission.

The Seed Shop

Here in a quiet and dusty room they lie,
Faded as crumbled stone or shifting
   sand,
Forlorn as ashes, shrivelled, scentless,
   dry –
Meadows and gardens running through
   my hand.

Dead that shall quicken at the trump of
   spring,
Sleepers to stir beneath June's morning
   kiss,
Though bees pass over, unremembering,
And no bird seek here bowers that were
   his.

In this brown husk a dale of hawthorn
   dreams;
A cedar in this narrow cell is thrust
That will drink deeply of a century's
   streams;
These lilies shall make summer on my
   dust.

Here in their safe and simple house of
   death,
Sealed in their shells, a million roses leap;
Here I can blow a garden with my breath,
And in my hand a forest lies asleep.

The Bishop's Candlesticks
Love and Mercy

Any story that ennobles or edifies the human spirit can be shared with the children. The opening sequence of *Les Misérables* is one such story and without destroying the plot, it is described here for dramatisation in school.

You will need the following characters

A Bishop
A housekeeper
An escaped convict
Chief of Police
Armed guard
Narrator

You will need the following props

2 silver candlesticks
a silver chalice
a bag
a dining room table and chairs
bread / food, etc.

Narrator
A prisoner escaped from jail, he was tired and hungry; cold and frightened. He had nowhere to go and no money. He was desperate for food and shelter.

> (*Enter convict, running across the stage, looking behind him in case anyone is following him.*)

Suddenly, the prisoner saw a light at a nearby house, so as he was desperate, he knocked on the door and asked for food, hoping that he would not be recognised as an escaped convict.

Prisoner
Please sir, help me, I have travelled a long way and I only want a little bread and water to sustain me for the rest of my journey.

Bishop
Come in, come in, out of the cold. I am sure that we can do better than bread and water.

Housekeeper, fetch this gentleman some hot food. Come and sit here by the fire and get yourself warm.

(Housekeeper enters with food.)

Bring some wine and serve it in our best silver chalice, for our visitor.

(The silver chalice is filled with wine. The prisoner eats hungrily and makes as if to leave.)

Bishop

My dear fellow, it is dark and cold outside, why don't you stay the night? Keep yourself warm by the fire. I must go to bed now, as I have to get up very early in the morning.

Prisoner

Oh thank you sir.

(Exit Bishop and Housekeeper.)

Cor, look at this lovely silver chalice, I know the old bloke's been kind, but if I steal this cup, I could sell it for a great deal of money. He won't miss it.

Narrator

The convict hid the chalice in his sack and left the house. Just as he was running away, he was seen by the Chief of Police and the armed guard who stopped him, searched him and arrested him. *(The action is mimed.)*

Chief of police

Stop thief, now you will hang. Open your sack, let's see what you've got inside. Oh I see, you stole this beautiful chalice from that kind old Bishop, did you, well we will soon see about that. Come along, let's see if the Bishop recognises you and can identify his chalice.

Narrator

The prisoner was frog-marched back to the Bishop's house. They knocked on the door.

Bishop

Hello officer, what can I do for you?

Chief of police

Do you recognize this wicked man?

Bishop

Why yes, of course I do, he spent the night here.

Chief of police

He might have spent the night here, but look how he has repaid you, he has stolen your beautiful silver chalice.

Bishop

Why officer, I meant him to have it. Young man, I meant you to have the candlesticks too, here you are, do take them.

Chief of police (aghast)
So he didn't steal them?

Bishop
No, no, of course not. Thank you, officer, for your help. Goodbye.

Narrator
The Chief of Police and the armed guard left the house, looking bewildered. When they had gone, the convict went down on his knees to the Bishop.

Prisoner
Thank you, thank you sir. But why did you help me like that? You know that I stole this cup from you, I was going to sell it to buy food.

Bishop
I know, and I meant you to have it and the candlesticks, really.

Prisoner
But why are you so kind to me, what do you want from me?

Bishop
The love and the mercy that I have shown to you, you must show to others. You will know what to do, when the time comes. The life I have given back to you, you must now give back to God. You do not owe me anything, but you do have a debt to God. Go and do good to someone else. Look out for ways to help someone as I have helped you today.

Prayer

O God, help us to show such love and forgiveness when others wrong us. Help us to spare one another and to show the sort of compassion that the Bishop showed to a common thief. Help us too, to find ways of helping others in need. Amen

Reflection

The man in the story stole precious items from a kind and generous Bishop. Think about stealing and how awful it must be for the victim of theft. Do you think the thief was sorry for his actions? Do you think he did try to repay the kindly Bishop by turning over a new leaf, doing good and helping others in need? What would you have done if you had been the Bishop? What would you have done if you had been the convict?

Hymn

No. 85, 'Spirit of Peace' in *Come and Praise 2*, BBC.

A Judge is Judged

This drama is based on an idea in *Divine Comedies* by Paul Burbridge and Murray Watts published by Monarch Publications, 1994.

You will need the following characters

Judge
God

You will need the following props

Judge's wig/or ridiculous alternative wig and handkerchief to place on top
Judge's brief-case and notes
List

This is the story of a Judge who dies and goes to Heaven and is waiting to be judged by God for his life on earth.

> *Judge*
>
> Well, I had better put my wig on, so He knows exactly who I am. (*Places wig on head. The more ridiculous, the better. Then places handkerchief on top of wig.*)
>
> Hello, helloo, is anybody there? I'm a most distinguished Judge, Lady Big-Wig. I'm very important. I've arrived in Heaven and I'm ready to be judged by God. Not that I've committed that many sins, you know. (*Consults fingernails.*) Oh deary me, no. But the people I've sent to prison – well they are very different, really. Murderers, thieves, traffic offenders – *I've* done nothing like that. No, no, I should get on alright when I'm judged today.
>
> Oh, dear, God is taking His time. I wonder what is He doing? Now let me just review my notes. How good have I been? Let me see. (*Opens brief-case and consults notes.*) Ah yes.
>
> Remember the Sabbath Day, to keep it Holy. Oh, yes, I've done that all right. Always been good on a Sunday, gone to church, read the right books, that kind of thing. Always kept Sundays Holy. Well, perhaps once and only once, mind you, I might have done a teeny-weeny bit of shopping at a Supermarket (*Gasp*), but I expect the Almighty Judge will understand. Now what else? Honour your Father and Mother. Yep, done that. Oh this is easy.
>
> You shall not kill – nope, I haven't killed anybody – well, not yet. You shall not bear false witness against your neighbour – what me, tell lies about someone else – no, never done that. Always proceeded on the basis of very good evidence. (*But thinks about this.*)
>
> You shall not covet; covet, I like this word. It means envy, feel jealous about, covet your neighbour's big house, or his flashy car, or his swimming pool, or his bean row or his sheep.

Well, I might have done a tincy-wincy bit of coveting, here and there, but nothing very serious. God won't find anything too naughty here.

Oh, good, I think I can see Him coming. I wonder if I ought to bow, people always used to bow to me in court, you know, as a sign of my extreme importance and respect for my high status. Funny, I didn't notice anyone bowing to me as I came through the gates today. I wonder why that was? Perhaps, *I* should bow? After all, He is the Almighty Judge. (*Half bows*.) I'll practice. (*Does a few curtsies and bows*.)

God

Do sit down. Er, you won't be needing this. (*Removes wig and puts it on his own head*.)

Judge

Oh no, of course not, Your Majesty. Silly me. You're the Judge here.

God

Now let me see (*Consults paper*).

Judge

I know that you know all about me, Your Majesty. So you will know already, that I've kept all your commandments on the list.

God

Ah, but I'm using the new list, as well as the old list.

Judge

New list, new list, what new list? I don't know anything about any *new* list. I've been sticking to the old list in my court. I've sent a lot of people down, I mean to prison, Sir, shown no mercy, you know the sort of thing. And *I* certainly haven't committed any of those guilty sins.

But don't worry, read me this new list, I'm sure I will have kept all these new rules as well. I was such a good judge, you see. (*Preens herself*.) Well, of course, I don't need to tell you that, you will know all about it already.

God

Yes, . . . and what about the sin of *Pride*?

Judge

Ah, er, um, Pride? Well. . . .

God

Yes and *Greed*?

Judge

(*Silence*) Oh.

God

Relationships with others? Have you always *Loved* others, as you have loved yourself? Gone that extra mile, turned the other cheek, given away some of your money to help those in need? You know the sort of thing.

Judge
(*Mmm*) Not exactly, no.

God
Now here is a very big item on the list. Have you always *Forgiven* others, as you yourself have been forgiven by me?

Judge
Well, um. . . .

God
Then how can your relationship with me be right, if your relationships with others are all wrong?

Judge
Oh dear, sorry!

Reflection

Think about the drama seen today and reflect on whether you are as forgiving, or as loving as you should be. Also, are we guilty of greediness and the wrong kind of pride? What is the right kind of pride? Think about what it means to go that extra mile, to turn the other cheek.

Prayer

Heavenly Father, help us to be very careful about judging other people's behaviour, when our own actions are often found to be even worse. Amen

Hymn

No. 1, 'A New Commandment I Give unto You, that You Love One Another' in *Mission Praise*, published by Marshall Pickering.

The Parable of the Talents

From P. Burbridge and M. Watts, *Time to Act*, Hodder and Stoughton, 1979 and reproduced with their kind permission. N.B. Permission for a *public performance* of this sketch should be obtained from P. Burbridge and M. Watts, PO Box 223, York YO1 1GW.

Acting this fun play demonstrates the need to use all the talents we possess in order to achieve our own peace. The story was originally told by Jesus, about a man who had three servants.

You will need the following characters

Two Narrators
Fred, a hardworking gardener
Ted, an astute salesman
Julian Potterton-Brown, a self-preoccupied fop
The Master, a stern but kindly landlord

(Note: *Choose one person, or two people, who are good at reading to read the Narrator's parts, indicated by One and Two. Alternatively, you could read the whole thing yourself, while the characters mime the actions. Give name tags to Fred, Ted and Julian, so that the assembled children can easily identify them.*)

One: Jesus told a story
Two: About
One: A man
Two: Who had
One: Three servants – for the sake of argument:
Two: Fred (*Pause while Fred enters and takes up position*),
One: Ted (*Pause while Ted enters and takes up position*),
Two: And Julian Potterton-Brown (*Longer pause while Julian Potterton-Brown makes a fastidious entrance*).
One: Now Ted was smarter than Fred
Two: But Fred was bigger than Ted.
One: Ted had a head to earn him his bread
Two: Which cannot be said for Fred.
One: But Fred often said:
Two: I don't 'ave Ted's 'ead
One: I manage wiv muscles instead.

Two: Now Julian Potterton-Brown

One: Was the odd one out.

Two: But this didn't deter him – after all:

One: 'I'm frightfully well-bred', he said.

Two: 'I'm greasier than Ted', he said.

One: 'I'm lazier than Fred', he said.

Two: 'And I don't rhyme with either of them, the creeps.'

One: One day their employer summoned them to his office. (*Enter the Master. He sits at a desk.*)

Two: Knock, knock.

One: 'Come in.

Two: Now listen you three

One: Fred, Ted and Julian whateveryourname is.'

Two: (*Julian prompting him*) 'Potterton-Brown.'

One: 'Granted.'

Two: 'Before I go away on my journey

One: I wish to give you each some money to look after.

Two: Form a queue, form a queue. (*Julian makes sure he gets to the front, but the Master bypasses him and goes straight to Fred at the end of the queue.*)

One: Five talents for you.

Two: Two talents for you. (*Given to Ted.*)

One: And one talent for you.' (*Julian looks at it disparagingly.*)

Two: So he waved goodbye.

One: He took his toothbrush.

Two: Took his hat.

One: Took his coat.

Two: Took his leave

One: And left. (*Exit Master.*)

Two: Now Fred had two thousand five hundred pounds.

One: Ted had one thousand pounds.

Two: Julian had five hundred pounds.

One: But what were they going to do with it?

Two: Fred had a flair for gardening and fancied growing some vegetables.

One: Ted had a flair for marketing and fancied his chances in business.

Two: Julian had flares and fancied himself.

One: Fred rolled up his sleeves

Two: Grabbed his money

One: And blew the whole lot on a spade

Two: A garden shed

One: A plot o' land

Two: A bag o' bulbs

One: An 'osepipe

Two: And a pair of wellies

One: And got stuck in.

Two: Ted surveyed the market very carefully.

One: Bided his time

Two: Picked his moment

One: Got his wallet

Two: Laid all his money on twenty

One: Second 'and camels.

Two: Julian was sensible

One: Was wise

Two: Was cautious

One: He considered the problems

Two: The pitfalls

One: The dangers that lay ahead

Two: The risk of losing everything.

One: And so Julian used his intelligence

Two: He thought

One: He planned

Two: He schemed

One: He did

Two: Nothing.

One: Nothing.

Two: But he was jolly careful with his money.

One: He wrapped it up in a silk handkerchief

Two: On a velvet cushion

One: In a little box

Two: And hid it under the floorboards.

One: And then:

Two: A few years later:

One: Knock, knock.

Two: Who's there?

One: Who do you think?

Two: The Master!

One: (*Gasping*) The Master!

Two: Quick, quick, form a queue, form a queue

One: Same to you

Two: Shut up

One: Shut up yourself.

Two: Ssssh!

One: Ssh!

> (*During this kerfuffle Julian has made sure, in contrast to the previous line-up, that he is at the back. The Master returns.*)

Two: And the Master called each man to account for the money he had entrusted to him.

One: 'Who's first?' (*Fred, finding himself at the front of the queue, reluctantly comes forward.*)

Two: 'Well, it's not as much as I'd hoped Master, cabbages got frostbitten last year . . .'

One: 'Never mind that – well done, good and faithful servant!

Two: You have doubled the money I gave you.

One: Enter into the joy of your Lord.

Two: Next.' (*Ted comes forward.*)

One: 'Yeah – well – er, second 'and camels – sold a few, bought a few, crashed a few – but you can't win 'em all, so 'ere you are.'

Two: 'Well done, good and faithful servant!

One: You too have doubled the money I gave you.

Two: Enter into the joy of your Lord.
One: Next.' (*Julian takes out a prepared speech.*)
Two: (*Loud cough.*)
One: (*Sound of clearing throat.*)

(*Julian applies a throat spray.*)

Two: 'Master!
One: My Lord!
Two: (*Ingratiatingly*) Master . . .
One: Knowing you to be a hard man etc., etc.,
Two: Blah blah blah, reaping where you did not sow
One: Blah blah blah, gathering where you did not winnow
Two: Ploughing where you did not . . . (*Fighting for words*) plough, and so on . . .
One: And so forth . . .
Two: I was afraid and hid the money.
One: I remain your obedient servant, Julian Pott—'

(*His speech is cut short by the Master snatching the paper from his hand and tearing it up. If the paper is mimed, one of the Narrators should make a suitable ripping noise.*)

Two: 'You did nothing!
One: You're all words.
Two: You're all talk.
One: All that I gave you has not grown one inch!
Two: Take away the talent and give it to the man who has ten.
One: And take this wicked servant and cast him into outer darkness.'

(*Julian is dragged off stage by invisible forces. The master turns, as if to address the audience.*)

Two: 'Don't be deceived.
One: Put everything that God has given you to good use.
Two: For one day you will have to give an account of your life
One: To him.'

Reflection

End the assembly with a time of quiet reflection on how we can best use the talents we have been given.

Hymn

No. 64, 'The Wise May Bring Their Learning' in *Come and Praise*, published by the BBC.

Further development

- Discuss with the children what they consider to be their talents.
- Perhaps draw up a chart or make a wall-frieze. Include some teachers' talents.
- Ask the children when and how they could use their talents.
- How could they improve their skills?
- Do the children know about the talents that other children in their class possess?

The Dragon at the Wedding

A Buddhist Tale

Adapted from a story told by Dharmachari Nagaraja and reproduced with his kind permission

You will need the following characters

Bride and Groom
Wedding guests
Servants (to serve the feast)
Children to hide beneath the table, to make the Dragon grow fat
A Buddhist Priest
A Dragon
Narrator

You will need the following props

Expanding dragon suit and mask
Long table covered with a cloth (under which children can hide, to make the
    dragon grow 'fatter' or 'thinner')
Food
Cornflakes (to tip over guests)
Best Seat (such as a carver or Teacher's chair)

Narrator
Once upon a time, there lived a huge Dragon. He was always on the prowl and would listen into everyone's conversations. He would grow very fat when people were greedy, or selfish, or were unkind to each other and hated one another or held bitterness in their hearts about something.

The only thing that would make the Dragon grow small or even disappear was when people were nice to each other or kind to one another, or co-operated with each other, or showed love to each other. He could not stand this.

The trouble was, that in this particular town, there was a lot of hatred and bitterness in people's homes and schools and places of work and so the Dragon would turn up uninvited and listen to all the nastiness going on and he would grow fatter and fatter, with glee.

One day a young couple decided to get married (*enter Bride and Groom*), and they were going to have a splendid wedding feast, to which everyone was invited. A long table was spread with delicious food and a special chair was set at the head of the table for the priest.

(Wedding guests arrive, all chatting, in their finery, to take their seats. Suddenly a dispute arises over who should sit in the best seat.)

First lady

I need to sit in the best seat, which is supposed to be for the Priest when he arrives, as I am the most important person at this wedding.

First man

(Roughly pushes lady out of the way.) No you can't sit there, I'm the most important person here today.

(Suddenly the Dragon makes his grand entrance and pushes both people out of the way and sits down in the best seat.)

Dragon

I love selfish people, yum, yum. They make me grow exceedingly fat and happy. *(Two children, hiding under the table, creep under the dragon's tail and expand his costume.)*

Second lady

Give me that food, I'm very hungry *(snatches food)*.

Second man

(Snatches food out of lady's hand.) NO, it's all mine, give it to me.

Dragon

Yum, yum, I love greedy people. *(Dragon grows even fatter as two more children come out from under the table and hide beneath his outfit.)*

Third lady

I don't know why the groom is marrying that lady, I hate her.

Dragon

Ooh! Hatred, I love a bit of hatred now and then. We are not supposed to hate anyone, but hatred makes me grow even fatter, lovely! *(Another child sneaks from under the table and hides beneath the Dragon's costume. The Dragon's tail should now have expanded across the stage with lots of pairs of feet underneath.)*

Third man

I can't forgive that boy, we've broken friends and I am never going to make it up ever. *(Stamps feet, crosses arms across his chest, pulls a face and sticks his tongue out.)*

Dragon:

Ooh!, I love bitterness, yummy, scrummy, in your tummy. *(Another child sneaks under the Dragon's costume.)*

(All the Guests push each other, snatch food, pretend to fight, throw cornflakes all over each other, until the Buddhist Priest enters.)

Narrator

Suddenly, a Buddhist Priest walked through the door and joined the wedding guests. *(Everyone freezes.)*

Buddhist priest

(To Dragon): You are *very welcome* to sit in the best seat, please do sit down there Sir, and make yourself most comfortable. I don't need the best seat at all. I am quite happy sitting anywhere, even on the floor.

Dragon

Oh dear, I don't like kindness or politeness, it makes me grow thin. *(One child sneaks out from under the costume and hides back under the table.)*

Second lady

Oh since the Priest is being kind and thoughtful, perhaps I'd better share some of my food. *(She turns to another guest.)* Would you like some jelly?

Guest

Oh thank you very much indeed. I love jelly. Weren't we silly to fight and squabble when there is plenty for everyone? We really ought to be kind and generous with what we have, and to share with those who have none.

Dragon

WHAT! Kindness, generosity, sharing FOOD, helping one another!? Oh no, I'm getting thinner, HELP! *(Another child sneaks out from under the Dragon's costume and hides underneath the table and the Dragon grows thinner.)*

Third lady

Do you know, the Bride is really very pretty, perhaps I could grow to love her.

Dragon

LOVE, love, can't have people loving each other. That is the last straw – ooh dear no, where would we all be if everyone started loving each other? There would be no more wars or fighting, no-one would get hurt, everyone might share what they had with each other, people might start looking after each other or they might even look after the planet or their animals. I simply can't have *love* in the world. Oh dear, what is happening to me, I'm losing weight. I'm getting thinner, I think I am disappearing. Heeelp! *(Dragon's tail is pulled back under the table until he completely disappears.)*

Narrator

It is a very strange thing, the Dragon only appears to spoil things when people are being nasty to each other and can't get on with one another; when they can't co-operate with each other or if they insist on their own way, or are hateful or greedy or spiteful. It is then that the Dragon appears and grows fatter and fatter with each bit of unkindness. So we must all make quite sure that the Dragon stays away from our school by being very loving and kindly and thoughtful and caring for one another. We must all try to be forgiving and share what we have and learn to co-operate with each other, so that the nasty Dragon is kept at bay.

Reflection

Sit very quietly and think about all the loving, kindly, helpful, truthful things that you could do today to keep the Dragon away from our school or classes or friendships.

Hymn

No. 99, 'Love will never come to an end', in *Come and Praise 2*, published by the BBC.

Poem

Read Kate Compston's poem printed below, 'Peace is like Gossamer', in *Leaves from the Tree of Peace* published by The United Reformed Church, 1989. Used with kind permission.

Peace is Like Gossamer

Peace is like gossamer –
vulnerable, yet indestructible:
tear it and it will be rewoven.
Peace does not despair.
Begin to weave a web of peace:
start in the centre
and make peace with yourself
and your God.
Take the thread outwards
and build peace within your family,
    your community
– and in the circle of those you find it hard
    to like.

Then stretch your concern
into all the world.
Weave a web of peace
and do not despair.
Love is the warp in the fabric of life:
truth is the weft:
care and integrity together –
vulnerable,
but ultimately
indestructible.
Together,
they spell
peace . . .

Kate Compston

Resources

Erricker, J., *Buddhist Festivals*, Heinemann, 1996.
Fossey, K., *Buddhism*, QED Publishing, 2007.
Ganeri, A., *The sound The Hare Heard and Other Stories*, QED Publishing, 2007.
Ganeri, A., *Buddhist*, Franklin Watts, 2003.
Ganeri, A., *Buddhist Beliefs and Cultures*, Franklin Watts, 1996.
Ganeri, A., *Wesak*, Heinemann, 2002.
Ganeri, A., *Buddhist Festivals Through The Year*, Franklin Watts, 2007.
Ganeri, A., *Buddhist Vihara*, A & C Black, 1998.
Ganeri, A., *Buddhist Stories*, Evans Brothers Limited, 2000.
Ganeri, A., *The Tipitaka and Other Buddhist Texts*, Evans Brothers Limited, 2003.
Geldart, A., *Let's Find Out About Buddhist Temples* Raintree Children's Book, 2005.
Knapp, B. & Magloff, L., *Buddhist Faith and Practice*, Atlantic Europe Publishing, 2005.
Knott, L. & Addiccabandhu, *My Buddhist Faith*, Evans Brothers Limited, 2003.
Magloff, L., *Buddhist Holy Days*, Atlantic Europe Publishing, 2007.
Magloff, L., *Buddhist Temple*, Atlantic Europe Publishing, 2005.
Marchant, K., *Great Religious Leaders: Buddha and Buddhism*, Hodder Wayland, 2005.
Penney, S., *Buddhism*, Heinemann, 1995.
Ross, M. *Holy Places: Bodh Gaya and Other Buddhist Holy Places*, Heinemann, 2003.
Senker, C., *I Am A Buddhist*, Franklin Watts, 2005.
Senker, C., *My Buddhist Year*, Hodder Wayland, 2003.
Thibault, D. et al, *The Prince Who Became A Beggar: A Buddhist Tale*, Moonlight Publishing, 1995.
Wallace, H., *Buddhism: Yuranan's Story*, Ticktock Media, 2006.
Wood, A., *Buddhist Temple*, Franklin Watts, 2005.

A Portuguese Symbol of Friendship

Is it not strange that Portugal's national symbol for welcome and friendship – a multi-coloured cockerel – should have been born out of a villainous desire for self-gain? The following play tells the story.

You will need the following characters

A tall cloaked stranger with a black bag
Innkeeper
Wicked servant
Two jailors
Mayor
Mayor's servant

You will need the following props

Black bag
Some 'silver' knives and forks; candelabra or goblets
Table and chairs
Cooked cockerel on a silver platter

Stranger
Innkeeper, I am on my way to the little town of Santiago de Compostela. Please can I have a meal and a room for the night?

Innkeeper
Certainly Sir, leave your bag here. I will get our waiter to serve you.

Servant
Sit down here, Sir. I will bring you some bread and wine. (*Serves food.*)

Stranger
My bag is heavy, can I leave it there until morning, Innkeeper?

Innkeeper
Certainly Sir, let me show you to your room.

(*When the pair leave the stage, the servant makes a big show of stealing the silver.*)

Servant

I am going to steal this silver, no-one will think that I have stolen it, they will think that it is the funny looking stranger who came here tonight. I will sell the silver and make lots of money, no-one will know it was me who stole it. Now, where can I hide the stuff for the time being? I know. I will put it in the stranger's bag. No-one will look for it there. (*Exit.*)

Innkeeper

Where has all my silver gone? (*Looks about, sees the bag.*) Aha – it's that stranger – he said his bag was heavy – he must have stolen it when no-one was looking. (*Looks in bag and holds up silver.*) Quick, send for the jailors, we have a thief staying at our inn tonight.

Enter two jailors

O.K., where is the thief? We will take him and put him in jail straight away. We will teach this stranger that we don't tolerate thieves in this village. The punishment for stealing here, is death by hanging.

(*The stranger is dragged out and handcuffed and frog-marched round the stage and then finally locked up in one corner of the stage.*)

Stranger

(*Pleads*) All men condemned to death are granted one last request. Will you please grant me one request?

First jailor

Depends what the request is.

Stranger

I request to be taken to see your Town Mayor, I have heard that he is a man of justice.

Second jailor

Seems a reasonable enough request.

(*They walk round the stage, before coming to rest at the Mayor's house. He is seated at a table eating his supper. The Jailors knock on the door, which is opened by the Mayor's servant.*)

Mayor's servant

Good evening, what do you want?

First jailor

We would like to see the Mayor urgently. This stranger is a thief and he will hang in the morning, but he has made one last request that he is allowed to see the Mayor tonight, before he dies.

Servant

But the Mayor is eating his supper, he cannot possibly be disturbed.

Second jailor

But we must see the Mayor tonight. This stranger will hang in the morning.

Servant

Oh very well, you had better come in, but make it snappy. I am just going to serve the Mayor's main course and he does not like his meal to get cold.

(The three go in front of the Mayor.)

Mayor

That was lovely soup, now where's the roast chicken that you have been promising me? Oh, who is this?

Servant

I will bring your supper in a moment, my Lord, but this prisoner has requested that you see him before he dies in the morning. He is accused of stealing.

Mayor

Very well stranger, your request has been granted. Now what did you want to say to me?

Stranger

My Lord, I was on a pilgrimage to Santiago de Compostela. I stayed the night at the inn here in Barcelos. I had not been in bed long, before the innkeeper called for these two jailors, because he accused me of stealing all his silver. But I swear, Sir, that I am innocent of this crime. I was on my way to worship God and was making a pilgrimage to the Church of St. James of Compostela. I swear by God and St. James that I am innocent of this theft and because this is the truth, my God and St. James will send you a sign to prove my innocence.

(Just at that moment, the servant enters with the cooked chicken on the platter and places it before the Mayor. As he does so, the cock crows. Everyone leaps to their feet aghast and points at the chicken and then at the stranger.)

Mayor

This man must be innocent, I have never heard a cooked chicken crow before. God knows that this man is telling the truth and He has given us this sign. We are the guilty ones. Guilty of wrongly accusing a man, just because he is a stranger. It is our own foolish pride that has prevented us seeing that the thief must be someone we all know well. As an indication that we are sorry for ill-treating a guest in our midst, I want you to put a picture of a cockerel in every household and every inn, as a sign of friendship and to remind us to welcome strangers. Let this man go free immediately and go and find the real thief.

Reflection

Reflect on how wrong it is to accuse someone of wrongdoing without knowing all the facts, just because that person has a different coloured skin, or religion or physical appearance.

Part 7

Peace in the Environment

7–11 Years Assembly

Kindness to Animals

The Brooke Hospital

Reverence for every living creature must be taught if there is to be peace in the animal world. The RSPCA produce a number of educational resources for schools (see address below). Children need to know that individuals can change the way animals are treated and perhaps bring them a special kind of peace.

A good way to introduce this whole subject is to mime Dorothy Brooke's story and her work with thousands of cavalry horses in Egypt in the 1930s. Today, there are many Brooke Hospitals/Clinics scattered all over the Middle East (see address below).

You will need the following characters

> Dorothy Brooke
> Major General Geoffrey Brooke (Dorothy's husband)
> Small committee of helpers
> Large group of children acting as 'sick' horses (horse masks)
> Group of owners with sticks
> Vet
> A number of Vet's assistants
> Narrator

Narrator
We are going to tell you about a courageous young woman called Dorothy Brooke and the wonderful work she initiated for old, sick and lame horses many years ago. We are also going to tell you about the work today and the establishment of many hospitals and clinics in her name around the world.

(Enter Dorothy Brooke with a suitcase.)

It was in October, in the year 1930, that Dorothy Brooke arrived in Cairo. She was utterly shocked by the sight of once magnificent cavalry horses, now suffering from terrible injuries and starvation.

(Enter horses who limp and collapse onto the floor.)

The British Government had sold twenty thousand of these wonderful creatures twelve years previously, to people in Egypt who could not afford to keep themselves, let alone their animals.

(Enter group of owners who beat their horses to get up.)

What she saw sickened her so much that she wrote a letter to the papers and suddenly money came flooding in from all sorts of people who wanted to help rescue these poor horses.

(Dorothy Brooke writes a long letter.)

Major General Geoffrey Brooke and a small committee of helpers used the money to buy back the remaining five thousand horses that were still alive and being made to work in Egypt.

(The Brookes and the committee take money to the owners and buy back the horses. The group then leads each horse away from their owners.)

Sadly, most of the horses had to be put down by the Veterinary Surgeon because it was the kindest thing to do in the circumstances. They were in such dreadful pain and they were suffering.

(The Vet gives most of the horses an injection, they go to sleep and are dragged off stage by a number of the Vet's assistants.)

The rest of the horses were fed and given proper stables, care and medical treatments. *(The action is mimed.)*

But the story does not end here. Dorothy Brooke decided to offer free veterinary services to all the working horses whose owners were so poor that they could not afford the Vet's fees and medicines, and who had no option but to work their poor horses until they literally dropped dead. In 1934, she opened the 'Old War Horse Memorial Hospital' or the 'Brooke Hospital for Animals' as it is now known. The hospital still treats thousands of sick horses with injuries and diseases and gives the owners a small allowance to help them to survive whilst their horses are in the hospital. If the horse is too sick to live, the Brooke Hospital buys the animal back from the owner and it is then given a few peaceful days before it is quietly put to sleep.

The Brooke Hospital also goes to outlying villages and markets to treat thousands of sick horses and donkeys that work the brick kilns. The Vets teach the people how to look after their animals properly and give them medicines to treat their ailments. In addition, the Brooke Hospital provides water troughs and shady shelters in many places, because these poor animals have to work in extremely high temperatures of over 38 degrees Centigrade (100 degrees Fahrenheit). New Brooke Hospitals/Clinics have opened in Jordan, Pakistan and India. Horses are treated for their diseases and they are re-shod by a farrier. Mobile vans take Vets and their helpers to many villages outside the hospitals, bringing relief to those poor animals that would otherwise not be able to receive treatment.

If you would like to help in this work, perhaps a collecting box could be put in each classroom for a week. Also, various items are provided for sale by the Brooke Charity, in order to raise funds for the Brooke Hospitals, shelters, water troughs and veterinary treatments. Perhaps a letter could be sent to parents to explain what the school is trying to do and why funds are needed.

Prayer

Father God, we thank you for the courageous work that was begun by Dorothy Brooke. We ask that you continue to use all sorts of people to help to bring relief to these poor horses and brick kiln donkeys.

Reflection

Think about the need to care for all animals everywhere that have been badly treated for whatever reason. What can we do to prevent this happening? How can we help? What are the basic needs that all animals have in common? Make a mental list.

Hymn

No. 80, 'All the Animals That I Have Ever Seen' in *Come and Praise 2*, published by the BBC.

Useful addresses

The Brooke Hospital for Animals
Broadmead House,
21 Paton Street,
London SW1Y 4DR
Tel: 0207 9300210
Web-site: www.thebrooke.org

RSPCA
Wilberforce Way
Southwater
Horsham
West Sussex RH13 9RS
Tel: 08703 335999
Web-site: www.rspca.org.uk

End the assembly with the poem 'Kindness to Animals' (Anon).

Kindness to Animals

Little children, never give
Pain to things that feel and live,
Let the gentle robin come
For the crumbs you save at home –
As his meat you throw along
He'll repay you with a song –
Never hurt the timid hare
Peeping from her green grass lair,
Let her come and sport and play
On the lawn at close of day –
The little lark goes soaring high
To the bright windows of the sky,
Singing as if 'twere always spring,
And fluttering on an untired wing –
Oh! let him sing his happy song,
Nor do these gentle creatures wrong.

Anon.

Conservation and Pollution
Cloacina's Story

This assembly is suitable for audience participation and is adapted by Elizabeth Peirce from the story 'What Now, Cloacina?' by Diane Edgecomb in *Spinning Tales, Weaving Hope* (Brody, E., *et al.*, eds) published by New Society Publishers, Philadelphia 1992.

You will need the following props

A flip chart and pen
A pebble

Storyteller
This is the story about Cloacina, a water spirit, pronounced Klo/a/chee/na. Can we all say her name? Let's have a practice. (*Assembled children repeat Cloacina's name . . . Klo/a/chee/na.*) Now I want you all to help me, whenever Cloacina says 'Oh no!' can you say, 'What's the matter Cloacina?' (*Another practice.*)

Cloacina
Oh no!

Children
What's the matter Cloacina?

Cloacina
Well, I just went into the woods for a little while and when I came back my huge lake had completely disappeared. Oh no!

Children
What's the matter Cloacina?

Cloacina
Look what I have found (holds up a pebble): it is a pebble from the bottom of my lake, but where has all my water gone? Oh no!

Children
What's the matter Cloacina?

Cloacina
There is a sign over there and a big pipe where my lake should be. I wonder what the sign says. Shall I spell it out for you? Perhaps one of you could read it for me. (*Writes on the flip chart*

. . . R – E – S – E – R – V – O – I – R) So my lake is called a Reservoir, but what *is* a Reservoir? Can anyone help me this time? (*Wait for answers and then*) Oh I see, it is a place where water is collected and then piped to homes and schools and factories. Well, don't tell me that all my water disappeared down that huge pipe to somebody's home or school or factory. People must have been using far too much water to make it *all* disappear. I think I should go down the pipe myself and investigate who it is that is using up all my water.

Storyteller
So off went Cloacina, down the long pipe. She could hear her voice echoing as she called out, 'Hello, is anybody there . . . hello, hello, hello, is anybody there . . . is anybody there . . .' She walked for quite a long time and found that the large pipe divided into several smaller pipes and then these smaller pipes divided into even tinier pipes, until eventually she saw a light at the end of the teeniest weeniest pipe. So she squeezed herself up and through a very tiny hole and landed in a slippery basin.

Cloacina
Oh, where on earth am I? This looks like a small basin and that looks like an enormous bath over there. But where can I be? Can anybody guess?

Children
In a bathroom!

Storyteller
Yes, in a bathroom, in someone's house.

Cloacina
Oh no!

Children
What's the matter Cloacina?

Cloacina
Surely all my water didn't get used up here in this one house? It must have been wasted by lots of people, using lots of water all over the town.

Storyteller
Just as Cloacina was wondering how her water could have been wasted, she heard the noise of children coming upstairs to wash themselves before going to bed. So she quickly hid behind the curtains and peeped around the edge to watch what they were doing. Three children burst into the bathroom and turned on all the taps at FULL SPEED. The water gushed down the waste pipes, whilst the children pushed and shoved each other to see who could wash first. Suddenly, there was another person in the bathroom. It was Dad and he sounded quite cross. 'I thought I told you children not to waste water?' he said. 'If you don't turn off the taps, all that water will go down the waste pipe, then the Reservoir will run dry.' 'Hmmmm', said Cloacina from her hiding place, 'hmmmm, hmmmm.' 'And there's something else,' said Dad, 'you are not to put anything poisonous down the drains either, no toxic paints or chemicals that are harmful to living things.' 'Hmmmm', said Cloacina from her hiding place, 'Hmmmm'. When the children had finally washed, being much more careful with the water

and making certain to turn off the taps when they did not need the water, Dad packed them off to bed and Cloacina said to herself, 'I think I should go and investigate what happens to all the wasted water.' So this time she climbed down the waste pipe which went into the drain pipe and then into another larger pipe and suddenly she was whisked along with tons of waste water from homes and schools and factories. It was a bit dirty and smelly. She was swished a long way to a place where the water was cleaned and finally, she was gushed out to sea.

Cloacina
Oh no!

Children
What's the matter Cloacina?

Cloacina
Well, I won't be able to find my Reservoir in the sea, will I? It's all been mixed up with the sea water!

Storyteller
Cloacina sat down on the sandy bottom of the ocean and started to cry, when suddenly, a very strange creature, with two powerful claws and eight spindly legs and large grey and green armour came by. Can you guess what sort of creature he was?

Children
(*Guess until the right answer is given.*) A lobster.

Storyteller
It was General Lobster and he was rolling a huge ball of rubbish in front of him. 'Out of my way, out of my way', he shouted at Cloacina. 'There is work to do.' 'What sort of work?', said Cloacina. 'We've got to clean up this ocean, look at the mess everywhere, bits of plastic and polystyrene, horrible stuff that is, it never dissolves you know, bits of old cars, bits of wood, chunks of tin – uggh – horrible creatures those land people, always chucking rubbish into my beautiful sea. And that's not all, they've started dumping poisonous stuff in my water and it's attacking my armour, look. Anyway, I can't stand here talking to you all day. I've got work to do. I'm going to try and stuff this ball of rubbish into that waste pipe over there, that will stop them messing up my sea and it will cause them a bit of trouble at their waterworks too. I must be off. Goodbye, goodbye.'

Cloacina
Before you go, can you tell me where my lake went to?

Storyteller
General Lobster said he didn't know, but told Cloacina to ask the Queen of the Sea, Queen Surf, who was just passing by on the crest of a wave.
   The Queen of the Sea told Cloacina that the only thing that would bring her lake back was preeeeecipitation and eeeeeeevaporation. But Cloacina said, 'What is preeeeecipitation and eeeeeeevaporation?' 'It means rain, in simple terms', the Queen said. 'Float up to the surface of the sea and you will see what I mean.' So Cloacina floated upwards and the sun warmed her through and through until . . .

Cloacina
Oh no!

Children
What's the matter Cloacina?

Cloacina
I'm feeling all tingly and light, I'm separating, hey I'm flying. I'm evaporating – I'm becoming water mist, ooogh!

Storyteller
Cloacina became so light that she floated up and back towards her lake, and as she did so, she gathered more and more pieces of mist around her until, when she was right above the place where her lake should be, she became part of a huge rain cloud that suddenly burst and began to fill up her lake once more. Cloacina was so happy, but she wondered as she floated comfortably home, how on earth she could keep her lake from disappearing again.

I wonder, children, if you could help me to remember what Cloacina had learned on her journeys? First of all, what did Dad tell the children? That's right, not to waste water and to turn the taps off when they were not actually using the water. What else did he tell them to do? Not to dump any poisons down the drain. Can you remember why? Because poisons harm all living creatures. What about the sea? We must be very careful not to dump any rubbish or poisons into the sea because it harms sea creatures. I think, if we all remembered to do this, it would make Cloacina and General Lobster very happy, don't you?

Poetry

Read the poem entitled 'Problems' by Brian Moses.

Problems

A voice was saying on Breakfast TV
how we should be taking more care
of our planet; and I thought between bites
of toast and jam, it really must
get untidy sometimes. I wondered
if God ever shouted out loud,
like mum when my room's in a dreadful state:
Hey, you lot, isn't it time
you set to work and tidied your planet?
Then another voice said, this world
is sick, and I wondered how he knew.
You could hardly feel its nose
like a dog, or shove a thermometer
under its tongue. Such problems were
far too complicated and I needed
expert advice, but my teacher
didn't know when I asked and joked that
she only knew where to look when
answers came out of a book. She told me,

instead, that my maths was a mess
and my handwriting wasn't tidy.
She didn't seem to understand,
I had bigger problems weighting my mind.

Brian Moses

Reflection

Think about the gift of water and the different ways in which it can be used. Reflect on how to save water and to use it economically. Think about not polluting our water systems and especially rivers and the sea. Think about not thoughtlessly discarding our rubbish when we are out. What *should* we do with it?

Prayer

Father God, help us to remember not to waste water, to conserve what we have and not to pollute our rivers and seas. Help us to remember that these places are home to many living creatures. Remind us to be careful with our rubbish too. Amen

Hymn

No. 76, 'God in His Love for Us Lent Us This Planet' in *Come and Praise 2*, BBC; or No. 15, 'Pollution Calypso' in *Every Colour Under the Sun*, Ward Lock.

Development

1   The children could try to record roughly how much water they use individually, in a day. (How many bowls full?) What do they use it for?
2   Ask the children to think of ways to *save* water. They could do a survey in school, to see how water is used and whether water is being wasted. How could they help to improve the situation?
3   Do some work with rain gauges, then ask the children to research rainfall in other countries and compare the effects on the different environments of the different amounts of rainfall.
4   Perhaps a visit to a Weather Station could be arranged or a walk round the nearest reservoir.

Rain Forests
The Tree Huggers

Based on a true story which took place on 26 March 1974 in an Indian village near the Tibetan border. The 'Chipko' Movement, or 'Hugging Trees' Movement, has stopped many large saw-milling companies from cutting down precious trees by mobilising local villagers to stand bravely in their path and hug the trees. Even in 2008, there is still a very real threat to the destruction of rainforests, with hundreds of acres of trees being felled to make way for more profitable crops, at the expense of many rare and endangered species and their habitats. This assembly is based on a story by David H. Albert called *Gaura Devi Saves Trees*.

The story can be retold using simple line drawings on an overhead projector.

You will need the following props

An overhead projector and screen
7 acetate sheets and pens

Gaura Devi was eight years old. She lived in an Indian village near the Himalayas. She and her mother used to collect dead twigs in the forest near their home in order to make fires on which to cook their food. They also used to pick the special plants, nuts and berries which grew under and around the trees. The animals and birds loved them too.

One day a truck arrived and many men with axes got out and started to walk towards the forest. Gaura Devi asked them what they were going to do. The men told her that the Forestry Commission had sold the whole forest and that they were going to cut the trees down.

Gaura Devi ran out of the forest as fast as she could and banged the huge gong in the centre of the village to summon the villagers and to warn them of the impending disaster.

Everyone stopped what they were doing at once, listened to what Gaura Devi had to say and then followed her to the forest. When they saw what the woodcutters were about to do, Gaura Devi's mother shouted to the big boss that if they tried to cut down the trees they would have to cut down the villagers first, because they were going to protect their forest. Gaura Devi's mother tried to explain that trees prevented soil erosion, protected the climate and most of all provided many natural resources.

The big boss shouted back to Gaura Devi's mother to get out of the way, but all the villagers, including the children, ran to the trees and put their arms around them in order to protect them from the axemen's blows.

The men tried to pull the children off the trees, but as fast as they did so, other villagers replaced them.

Finally, the men gave in and returned to the city. Later on, an important group of experts visited the forest and as a result of their report, the Government placed a ten-year ban on all tree-felling in that area of Northern India. So the villagers had won their battle and the trees were protected.

Follow-up work

1   Go out and hug all the trees in and around the school.
2   Explain the importance of trees in the environment.
3   Identify and draw as many different species as possible, make a 'Tree' book.
4   Learn about tree products. What comes from trees, what is made of wood, how can we conserve our resources? Set up a 'wooden' display.
5   Plant a tree or grow trees from seeds.
6   Watch the video called *The Man who Planted Hope and Grew Happiness*, the true story of a man who spent forty years of his life planting trees, through two world wars, in Southern France.

Prayer

Father God, you have provided us with magnificent trees of every kind. Help us to be protectors of trees rather than wasteful with your natural provision. May we never damage trees. Keep us mindful not to waste tree products such as paper. Amen

Hymn

No. 6, 'The Earth is Yours, O God'; or No. 1, 'Morning Has Broken'; or No. 3, 'All Things Bright and Beautiful', all in *Come and Praise I*, BBC.

Poetry

Read the poem below entitled 'New Responsibility,' by Kate Compston, in *Threads of Creation* published by The United Reformed Church, 1989. Used with kind permission.

New Responsibility

Great Spirit,
still brooding over the world –
We hear the cry of the earth,
we see the sorrow of land
raped and plundered in our greed
for its varied resources.

We hear the cry of the waters,
we see the sorrow of stream and ocean
polluted by the poisons
we release into them.

We hear the cry of the animals,
we see the sorrow of bird, fish and beast
needlessly suffering and dying
to serve our profit or sport or vanity.

Please teach us
a proper sensitivity
towards your feeling creation,
a proper simplicity
in the way we live in our environment,
a proper appreciation
of the connectedness of all things,
a proper respect
for the shalom of the universe.

We turn from our arrogant ways
to seek you again, Lord of life.
Redeem us – and redeem your world
And heal its wounds and dry its tears.
May our response to you bear fruit
in a fresh sense of responsibility
towards everything you have created.

Recycling
The Tailor's Story

Before telling the following tale, discuss recycling and waste and what the children can do about it in their own small way. Perhaps different classes could keep records of what they recycle and how each item is re-used. There is a useful address at the end of the assembly for recycling good-quality books to send to those children who have none.

The Tailor

Long ago, there lived a very poor tailor who spent his life making overcoats for other people. The poor tailor desperately needed a new overcoat himself, but he never had enough time or money to spare to make himself one.

One day a very rich man came to see him and asked the tailor to make him a new coat out of the latest fashionable material. 'But there is nothing wrong with your old coat', exclaimed the poor tailor. 'I'm tired of it,' the rich man explained, 'I don't like the colour, it's out of date and I fancy a new one.' 'But it is such a pity to throw this one away,' said the poor tailor. 'I don't know why you are complaining,' said the rich man, 'I shall pay you very well to make me a new coat.'

'All right,' said the tailor, 'but may *I* have your old coat, when I have made you this new one?' The rich man agreed to give the tailor his old coat and so the tailor set to work to make the rich man a new one. When the tailor had finished the new coat and had been paid very handsomely for his trouble, he set to work very carefully, to alter the rich man's old *coat* to fit himself. When he had finished the work, the tailor loved the coat so much that he wore it and wore it until the coat was really worn out. Or was it? The tailor thought that if he carefully *re-cut* the coat, cutting out the worn pieces and sewing together the good pieces, he could make himself a smart new *jacket*. This he did and he loved the jacket so much that he wore it and wore it until the jacket finally wore out. Or did it? The tailor thought if he carefully *re-cut* the jacket and cut out the worn areas, he could make himself a smart new *waistcoat*. This he did and he loved his waistcoat so much that he wore it and wore it until finally the waistcoat became completely worn out. Or was it? The tailor decided that if he carefully cut out the worn areas he could *re-model* the waistcoat into a *cap*. This he did and he loved his cap so much that he wore it and wore it until it finally became so threadbare that he decided that he could wear it no longer because it was completely and utterly worn out. Or was it? The tailor thought and thought how he could re-cycle his cap so as not to waste the material. There was so little material of any use left now. But suddenly, he had a bright idea. He desperately needed a new top button for his shirt, so very carefully, he cut a piece of fabric from the worn cap and managed to make a *button* with it. He wore this button every day until finally the button wore out. Or did it? The tailor found that there was just enough of the button left to make a *story* which he told me and now I'm telling you! Can you tell someone else and re-cycle the story?

'The Tailor' is based on a story by Nancy Schimmel in *Just Enough to Make a Story: A Source Book for Storytelling*, Sister's Choice, 1992. Ms Schimmel based her story on a Yiddish folk song.

Prayer

Father God, we are conscious that we have so much, whilst many people have so little. Help us to be more caring about our planet and its inhabitants. Help us to re-use materials whenever possible and so reduce the amount of waste and resources that we need to use. Amen

Reflection

Take time to think about how we can be better citizens by re-cycling rather than dumping our rubbish.

Hymn

No. 17, 'Milk Bottle Tops and Paper Bags', in *Someone's Singing, Lord*, published by A & C Black.

Useful address

Book Aid International
39–41 Coldharbour Lane
London SE5 9NR

Tel: 0207 7333577
e-mail: info@bookaid.org
web-site: www.bookaid.org

Toxic Waste
Peace for Some, Injury for Others

This play is based on a true story. It was a most sad and brief news item broadcast in the Spring of 1993. A rich country had dumped some toxic waste on a very poor country. It was found by some peasant farmers who spread the deadly waste on their vegetable gardens, believing the waste to be vegetable fertiliser. The children of the farmers became very sick, had headaches and some died. Many adults, too, became ill and died. To educate children today about the dangers of dumping toxic waste may provide the voices of protest tomorrow.

You will need the following characters

A group of waste-disposal experts in white coats and masks
A group of poor farmers
A group of poor children
A group of poor parents
Narrator

Narrator
Today we are going to act out a play, based on a true story about the dreadful consequences of dumping chemical waste on innocent and poor people. Chemical/toxic waste is produced by industrial societies in their manufacturing processes. That is, in the making of plastics and consumer goods like televisions and in the making of petrochemical products, etc. Toxic waste includes chemicals like cyanide, solvents, asbestos, pesticides and metals like cadmium and mercury. Some waste is dumped in landfill sites or in the sea, or taken to countries that will accept large shipments of waste, for payment of large fees.

First waste-disposal expert
Right, you men, you had better cover your heads, hands, faces and bodies before you shift this deadly stuff. Here you are, put on your face masks, protective suits, gloves and boots.

(The action is mimed. The group of waste-disposal experts put on their protective garments.)

Second expert
We have been given permission by this foreign government to dump the drums in that field over there. There is a large agricultural shed in that field. We can lock the shed up and the stuff will be quite safe. If anybody asks you what you are doing, just tell them you are storing some governmental stuff, O.K.?

Narrator

The men rolled the barrels off the ship and dragged them across the field to the agricultural shed. (*The action is mimed.*)

Third waste-disposal expert

Right, line up the drums in rows of twelve by twelve. That's it, make a new line, pile them on top of one another. I'll be back to lock up the shed when you have finished. (*The action is mimed.*)

Narrator

The men worked all day, storing the drums of deadly poison. Then the waste-disposal experts took out a large lock and locked the main doors of the shed. As they were doing this, a small group of farmers appeared to watch them.

First farmer

Hey, what have you put in our shed? We usually store our vegetables in there.

First waste-disposal expert

Don't worry, it's nothing, we are just storing some drums for your government. You must not touch them. They belong to the government, do you hear? It's very important stuff, you will be in trouble if you touch the drums.

Narrator

The waste-disposal experts finished what they were doing, packed up their belongings and returned to their ship. The group of farmers were intrigued by this secretive horde. They began to peer through the cracks in the walls of the shed to try and see what was inside.

Second farmer

Oh look, I can see, I can see, there are dozens of drums inside. What are they for, do you think?

Third farmer

Let me look. Oh yes, I can see them. They look like drums of fertiliser to me. I've seen drums like these being unloaded at the docks, by that huge agricultural firm.

Fourth farmer

We had better leave them alone, I expect the government will be sending their officials along soon to collect the drums and spread the fertiliser on the land in order to get huge crops to sell in foreign countries.

Narrator

Time went by, and nobody came to collect the drums or to distribute the contents. The shed began to fall into disrepair, so much so, that it was easy for men or children to get into the shed. The farmers who had first seen the waste-disposal experts thought that the drums had just been forgotten about and that the contents were going to be wasted.

First farmer

Well, the Government Officials have never collected their fertiliser; look, the drums are beginning to rot and the fertiliser is just wasting away.

Second farmer
We couldn't afford to buy expensive stuff like this. We might as well use it on our vegetable patches as leave it here to rot. I saw a programme once about using fertiliser and it made the plants grow twice the size, you know.

Narrator
So the farmers worked all day to spread the 'fertiliser' around their vegetables. (The action is mimed.) When the vegetables were ready for harvesting, the potatoes and green vegetables, tomatoes and salad things, the farmers took them home to their families. Meals were prepared by parents and served to the children and babies.

(The action is mimed; parents giving bowls of food to the children; eager happy faces turn into faces contorted with pain and agony, as one by one the children eat and fall sick. The play ends at this point with adults and children frozen into agonised shapes.)

The whole play can be made more effective if the children, in silence, carry placards across the stage, cataloging the Toxic Waste Disasters that have taken place in recent history.

- 1984 Bhopal, India: a pesticide leak from a factory kills 2,500 people. Many more people suffered injuries to their eyes and lungs.
- 1986 Chernobyl, Soviet Union: an explosion at the nuclear power station caused radioactive material to escape and drift all over northern Europe. Many people, close to the disaster, became ill and died.
- 1986 River Rhine, Germany: factory fire causes 30 tonnes of toxic waste to be washed into the river, killing everything along the river banks for many miles.
- 1989 The *Exxon Valdez* oil tanker disaster off Alaska: the huge oil tanker hit rocks off the Alaskan coast, spilling millions of gallons of oil and killing hundreds of thousands of birds, fish, seals and otters.
- 1990 Ufa, USSR: a leak of phenol from the pesticide factory; 600,000 had to be evacuated.
- 1991 Livorno, Italy: an explosion on an oil tanker in the harbour killed 140 people and caused much pollution in the area.
- 1992 Guadalajara, Mexico: a gas explosion in the city sewers killed 210 people and injured 1,500 people.
- 2001 AZF (France's largest fertiliser manufacturer): explosion at the Toulouse chemical factory; 31 dead, 2,442 injured.
- 2002 Lagos, Nigeria: armoury explosion; 1,100 killed, dozens injured.
- 2005 Jilin, China: chemical plant explosions; 6 killed, tens of thousands of residents evacuated.
- 2006 Ilado Pipeline explosion near Lagos, Nigeria: 150 killed.

The Sydney Tar Ponds and Coke Ovens sites in the city of Sydney, Nova Scotia, Canada, are known as the largest toxic waste site in North America.

Further development

Children can further research these incidents and many others via the web-site: www.wikipedia.org/list of disasters. What more can they find out about each event? What have been the long-term consequences?

Reflection

In a moment of quiet, think about all the innocent people caught up in these accidents. Do we consider what we throw away and who might be harmed?

Prayer

Father God, make Governments and those in authority aware of the dangers of toxic waste and use every possible means to protect the innocent and the vulnerable from harm. Amen.

Hymn

No. 83, 'I'm Going to Paint a Perfect Picture', in *Come and Praise 2*, published by the BBC.

Pollution/conservation information books

Amos, J., *Pollution*, Watts Books, 1995.
   Other books in this excellent series include: *Rainforests, Animals in Danger*; *Waste and Recycling*; *Feeding the World*.
Baines, J., *Oceans* (Our Green World Series), Wayland, 1992.
Bellamy, D., *How Green are You?*, Frances Lincoln, 1991.
Bennett, P., *Earth, The Incredible Recycling Machine*, Wayland, 1993.
Bright, M., *The Greenhouse Effect*, Franklin Watts, 1991.
   Also written by M. Bright: *Pollution and Wildlife*; *The Ozone Layer*; *Traffic Pollution*; *Polluting the Oceans*; *Acid Rain*.
Church, D., *Protecting the Environment*, Franklin Watts, 2001.
   Excellent ideas for encouraging children to help protect the environment.
Collinson, A., *Repairing the Damage. Pollution*, Evans Bros Ltd., 1997.
   An excellent historical overview of the planet and a clear time-line of nuclear bomb tests; water pollution maps; air pollution, Chernobyl. Contains a useful glossary.
Drum, J. and Sutton, H., *Living with Nature: Watch Book of Conservation*, BBC, 1987.
Edmonds, A., *Acid Rain* (Closer Look At Series), Franklin Watts, 1996.
   Series includes *The Ozone Layer*; *The Rainforest*; *The Greenhouse Effect*.
Gordon, M., *Why Should I Save Water?*, Hodder Wayland, 2001.
   Also included in the series: *Why Should I Protect Nature?*;
   Why Should I Recycle?; *Why Should I Save Energy?*
Green, J., *Rainforests At Risk*, Chrysalis Children's Books, 2005.
Green, J., *Learn About Rainforests: A Fascinating Fact File*, Lorenz Books, 2000.
Hare, T., *Acid Rain: Save Our Earth*, Franklin Watts, 1990.
   Also written by T. Hare: *Vanishing Habitats*, 1991; *The Greenhouse Effect*; *Polluting Air*; *The Ozone Layer*, 1992.

Harlow, R. and Morgan, S., *Nature at Risk*, Kingfisher Books, 1995.

Harlow, R. and Morgan, S., *Pollution and Waste*, Kingfisher Books, 1995.

Horton, P. *et al.*, *Earth Watch*, BBC Books, 1992.

Ingpen, R. and Dunkle, M., *Conservation*, Michelle Anderson Publishing, 1992.

Jennings, T., *People or Wildlife*, A & C Black, 1992.
  This is a really excellent book.

Knapp, B., *Caring for Our Environment*, Atlantic Europe Publishing Co. Ltd., 2004.
  Covers questions like, why do animals become extinct? Endangered species, saving energy, water, recycling waste, pollution, etc.

Kozak, M., *Greenpeace*, Heinemann, 1998.

Lambert, D., *Pollution and Conservation*, Wayland, 1988.

MacQuitty, M., *Oceans* (Eyewitness Guides), Dorling Kindersley, 2003.

McGovern, A., *Too Much Noise*, Houghton Mifflin, 1995.

Morgan, S., *Acid Rain*, Franklin Watts, 2005.

Nelson, N., *Conservation* (Starting Geography Series), Wayland, 1992.

Penny, M., *Pollution and Conservation*, Wayland, 1988.

Pollock, S., *The Atlas of Endangered Places*, Belitha Press Ltd., 1993.
  This is a really excellent book and very useful for classroom research.

Powell, J., *Caring for the Environment*, Wayland, 1997.

Smith, V., *I Can Help Clean Our Air*, Franklin Watts, 2001.
  Also in the series: *I Can Help Recycle Rubbish*; *I Can Help Save Water*; *I Can Help Protect Nature*; *I Can Help Weather Watch*; *I Can Help Save Energy*.

Sneddon, R., *Rainforests* (Reprint pending), Franklin Watts, 2004.

Thomas, H. & Thompson, S., *The Conservation Project Book*, Hodder & Stoughton, 1990.

Walker, J., *Man-made Disasters: Oil Spills*, Watts Books, 1993.

Woodward, J., *Oceans*, Hodder Wayland, 2004.

War and Peace Stories

The Last Snowflake

This assembly is an adaptation of 'The Weight of a Snowflake' in *New Fables, Thus Spoke the Carabou* by Kurt Kauter. It is a dance-mime to demonstrate that one person's action does count for something. The last snowflake is a symbolic representation for one more voice. One more voice may be all that is lacking to change a violent situation into a peaceful one. Never underestimate the power of one more voice of protest.

You will need the following characters

Narrator
Mouse (brown ears and tail)
Dove (white wings)
10–12 Snowflake dancers (crêpe-paper skirts; white vests; tinsel in hair)
Last Snowflake

You will need the following props

Branch of a fir tree (made out of a long line of tights stuffed with newspaper; fir tree fronds sticking out)
Taped music to which Snowflakes can dance

> *Narrator*
> Jesus said, 'Blessed are the peacemakers'. But have you ever thought how difficult it is to speak out and be a peacemaker? If you see and hear a quarrel going on, you might be tempted to stand and watch, rather than to get involved, or turn away when you see someone fighting, rather than try to be a peacemaker. The story that we are going to tell you today shows just how one action may be all that is needed to change a situation.
> The story is about a mouse who asks a dove what is the weight of a snowflake.
>
> *(Enter mouse and dove.)*

Mouse
'Can you tell me what a snowflake weighs?'

Dove
A snowflake weighs nothing, absolutely nothing at all.

Mouse
Then I must tell you a most remarkable story. When I was sitting on this fir tree branch today, it began to snow, very gently, you know.

> (*Snowflake dancers enter and dance to taped music. Each Snowflake comes to rest on the branch next to the mouse.*)

Mouse
(*Continues with his story.*) I decided to count the snowflakes that fell onto my branch. One, two, three . . . (*Mouse counts the 'frozen' dancers*). And do you know, I counted two million and twenty-two snowflakes.

Dove
Wow, did you really?

Mouse
Well, when the very next snowflake fell onto my branch, two million and twenty-three, its weight, as you have said, which was nothing, absolutely nothing at all, well that last snowflake made the whole branch break off the tree.

> (*The last snowflake enters, dances round and comes to rest on the branch. As it does so, there is a loud crack and the other snowflakes sink to the floor and lie motionless.*)

Dove
Well, you do surprise me. Perhaps one does count for something after all. Perhaps one is all that is needed to make the difference to any situation.

Narrator
I think one counts for something too, don't you? Perhaps one *more* voice is all that is needed to bring about Peace in any situation. 'Blessed are the Peacemakers.'

Reflection

Think about ways you could make a difference this week. If we were to act together, think how we could change war into peace; lost into found; disappeared into re-appeared.

Hymn

No. 145 'O Let us Spread the Pollen of Peace Throughout the Land' in *Come and Praise 2*, BBC.

Paul's Armour
War and Peace

For this assembly you will need some visual aids: body armour, belt, leather shoes / leggings, shield, helmet, sword. (See pp. 148–50 for diagrams and instructions for making a cardboard helmet, sword and shield for a typical Norman knight.)

Alternatively, any slides or pictures from the Bayeux Tapestry will provide a clear guide to the arms and armour worn by a Norman knight at the time of the Battle of Hastings, in 1066. Start by reading Ephesians chapter 6, verses 13–18. The idea behind this assembly is to show and contrast a soldier's armour required for war, with Paul's armour required for Peace. Of course, Paul would have referred to the armour of a Roman solider for his illustrated message and so if the teacher can obtain pictures/artefacts for a Roman soldier, the same points can be made. Prior to this assembly, the teacher needs to give the children some idea of who Paul was; perhaps the story of his conversion could be told (see Acts chapter 9).

Mail shirt

War

The Norman knight needed protection in battle. The mail shirt was made of inter-linked steel rings and gave a certain degree of protection against the sword slash or the lance thrust by his opponent. It was worn over a padded under-garment. It was a flexible piece of armour, allowing the wearer to move easily in battle.

Peace

Paul said Christians needed to put on the '*Shirt of Righteousness*'; that is, we are to be right-minded, to be honest, to be honourable, fair, to be on our best behaviour, to have integrity, to be good, to lead good lives, to set a good example, to hate wrong. This armour would always protect us in difficult times.

Belt

War

The soldier needed a very strong belt to go around him completely. It had to be made of very strong leather to hold the sword and the scabbard. It was no use having a flimsy belt, that would break or fall off, because the soldier might need to withdraw his sword at any time to protect himself.

Peace

By contrast, Paul said we must put on the belt of '*Truth*'. Truth must surround us, and when you think about it, truth should surround everything that we do at home, at school, at work. Do you put on the belt of truth, every day? Do you promise to tell the truth, even when it is difficult and may result in punishment? We must be truthful, in all that we say and do. If we find something that does not belong to us, the truthful thing to do is to tell someone, so that it can be returned to the rightful owner. Grown-ups have to tell the truth too. Witnesses have to tell the truth about what they saw (discuss a current newspaper story), and even very young children may be called upon to be witnesses, so therefore we must learn to tell the truth always.

Leather shoes / leggings

War

The well-armed warrior was only as good as the shoes he wore, because he needed to get *to* the battle, as well as fight *in* the battle. If he did not have good shoes, and stones cut his feet, he would hobble and his enemy would have the advantage and could strike a lethal blow. He may have to walk many miles. He would certainly be on his feet for a very long time, and so he needed to be comfortable, and protected from rocky ground, etc. In other words, he needed to be well-shod.

Peace

Paul said we, too, must be well-shod with the '*Shoes of Peace*', so that wherever our feet take us, we must take the message of Peace. Jesus preached this message too and he was the supreme example of a man of peace. When he was spat upon, whipped, made fun of, had his clothes torn, and cruel thorns stuck into his head, he did not fight back. He could have done. He certainly could have brought down all his powers to wipe out his persecutors, yet he did not. He had been teaching his disciples to love their enemies, turn the other cheek, not to repay evil for evil; but to be kind to those who were horrible (see Luke 6:27–38).

He was trying to say that Peace starts with us, you and me, not trying to get our own back or take revenge. When somebody does something wrong to us, we must remember the gospel of peace. Peace could reign in Iraq, if people said, 'I am for peace', 'I'm not going to take any more revenge', 'I am not going to hit back'.

Kite-shaped shield

War

As a piece of armour in war, the kite-shaped shield would have given the mounted warrior a good deal of protection, because it curved around his body to protect him from the weapons of his opponents.

Peace

Paul said that we also needed a shield to protect us; a shield of '*Faith*' that we can wrap around ourselves in times of trouble. Now each one of us, whether we are young or old, meets trouble at some time or other in our lives. If someone tells you that he has led a trouble free life, then he is not telling you the truth. So what do we do in times of trouble? If you do not have the shield of faith, then you have to rely upon yourself. This can be a pretty empty experience, if there is no-one there to help you. But Paul taught that if you believed in God and had the shield of faith in God, you could pray to Him to help you and protect you.

Helmet

War

The warrior in battle needed, above everything else, protection for his head. The conical-shaped helmet was designed to deflect blows away from the head and body. (Demonstrate this point by showing how a sword slides off a conical-shaped helmet.) In other words, the helmet saved the soldier from certain death.

Peace

Paul taught that the helmet of 'Salvation' was also designed to remind us of this fact. In other words, if we put on the helmet of salvation, we would be saved from certain death. Jesus taught that all those who believed in Him would have this 'salvation' or eternal life. He broke the power of death, He rose from the dead three days after He had been crucified. So Paul taught that if we put on the helmet of salvation we would be saved from death.

Sword

War

As an instrument of war, the sword played the most important part. It was the means by which the soldier inflicted injury or death upon his opponent.

Peace

Paul taught us that we should take up 'God's word' as our imaginary sword. This would be our most powerful weapon. God's word is the Bible and Paul was trying to show that the Bible has all the answers, as to the way we should live our lives.

Draw all the threads together by using a picture of a knight and placing large labels for the children to read beside each item of dress, i.e.

Mail shirt   = Righteousness
Belt   = Truth
Leather shoes = Gospel of Peace
Shield   = Faith
Helmet   = Salvation
Sword   = God's Word

Leave the picture in place and ask the children daily if they can remember the message.

Reflection

Think about how we can prepare ourselves for each day as we dress in the mornings. For instance, are we going to put on the belt of truth and the shoes of peace?

Prayer

Father God, help us to try each day to put on Paul's imaginary armour for peace. Amen.

Hymn

No. 147, 'Make Me a Channel of Your Peace' in *Come and Praise 2*, BBC.

Poetry

Read the poem below, 'Peace Comes' by George de Gay.

Peace Comes

Peace comes, when we feel right inside,
When we've been fair, whate'er betide.
Though others blame, though others
   scoff,
Peace comes.

Peace comes, when we, for love not gain,
Have helped another take life's strain.
With friendly smile or kindly deed,
Peace comes.

Peace comes when we have stood the
   test,
When tempted, we have come out best.
When all unruliness has fled,
Peace comes.

Peace thus arises in each heart,
When fellow-feeling plays full part.
When we our harmful passions tame,
Peace comes.

Peace does not come from outward
   things,
But when the seed from which it springs,
Is freely sown by anyone,
Peace comes.

When thus mankind has sown its field,
A blessed harvest it will yield,
A truly holy harvest home,
When peace comes.

George de Gay in *Voices Speaking Peace*,
an anthology of poems and prayers by Unitarians,
published by The Unitarian Peace Fellowship, 1990
(reproduced with the kind permission of the author).

Development

Using the diagrams overleaf, let the children make their own helmets, shields and swords out of cardboard, silver foil, paints, glue, etc.

How to make a Norman helmet

Based on a construction by I. G. Peirce, first published in 'Domesday 900, Winchester; Information Pack for Teachers'.

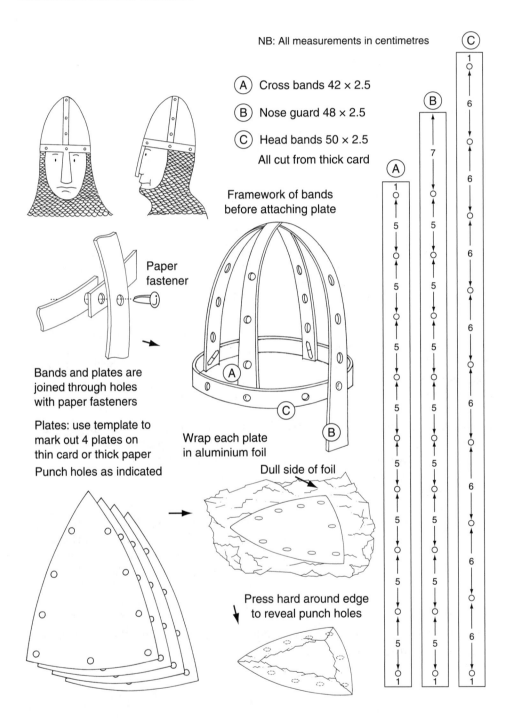

NB: All measurements in centimetres

(A) Cross bands 42 × 2.5

(B) Nose guard 48 × 2.5

(C) Head bands 50 × 2.5

All cut from thick card

Framework of bands before attaching plate

Paper fastener

Bands and plates are joined through holes with paper fasteners

Plates: use template to mark out 4 plates on thin card or thick paper

Punch holes as indicated

Wrap each plate in aluminium foil

Dull side of foil

Press hard around edge to reveal punch holes

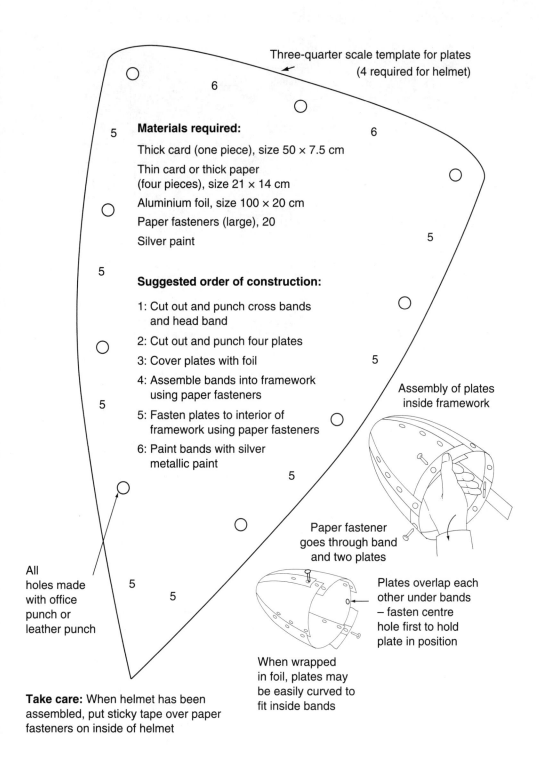

Three-quarter scale template for plates
(4 required for helmet)

Materials required:

Thick card (one piece), size 50 × 7.5 cm

Thin card or thick paper
(four pieces), size 21 × 14 cm

Aluminium foil, size 100 × 20 cm

Paper fasteners (large), 20

Silver paint

Suggested order of construction:

1: Cut out and punch cross bands
   and head band

2: Cut out and punch four plates

3: Cover plates with foil

4: Assemble bands into framework
   using paper fasteners

5: Fasten plates to interior of
   framework using paper fasteners

6: Paint bands with silver
   metallic paint

Assembly of plates
inside framework

Paper fastener
goes through band
and two plates

Plates overlap each
other under bands
– fasten centre
hole first to hold
plate in position

All
holes made
with office
punch or
leather punch

When wrapped
in foil, plates may
be easily curved to
fit inside bands

Take care: When helmet has been
assembled, put sticky tape over paper
fasteners on inside of helmet

How to make a kite-shaped shield and a broad sword

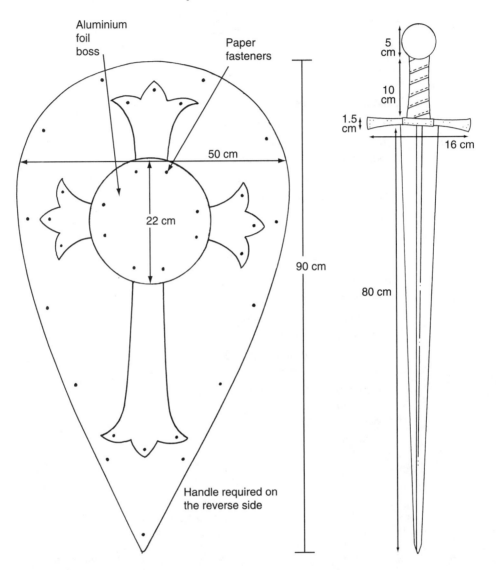

Aluminium foil boss

Paper fasteners

5 cm

10 cm

1.5 cm

16 cm

50 cm

22 cm

90 cm

80 cm

Handle required on the reverse side

Materials required:

Thick card (one piece), size 50 × 90 cm

Thin card circle, size 22 cm diameter

Cover circle with aluminium foil

Fix to shield with glue or paper fasteners

Materials required:

One piece of thick card for the blade, and grip, size 90 cm (blade 80 cm, plus grip 10 cm). Card for the crossbar, size 16 cm", to be glued across blade. Double circular disc of card for the pommel, diameter 5 cm, to be glued onto the grip.

Picture Books
War and Peace

There are so many lovely picture books that can be used as starting points in an assembly. A few are listed in the following pages; three are described in detail below. Mostly, the books below are intended for use with 5–7 year olds, but they can be used equally successfully with older children, who will appreciate the meaning at a deeper level.

Scholes, K., *Peacetimes*, Belitha Press, 1997.
  Peacetimes explores what peace means to different people, like 'a cup of hot chocolate on a winter's evening', and how problems can be resolved through discussion, working together, listening to one another. The role of the peacemaker is discussed and the complicated issue of being 'at peace' amidst turbulence is raised. The book also poses lots of thought-provoking questions for discussion and children will have their own individual answers.

Innocenti, R., *Rose Blanche*, Red Fox, 2004.
  This book, more suitable for 7–11 year olds, is about the outbreak of the Second World War in Germany. Rose Blanche discovers that there are children in the trucks that rumble through her town. She is determined to find out where the children are being taken and, having discovered the horrors of a concentration camp, the story unfolds around Rose Blanche's own response to what she sees. This is a thought-provoking book on the vicissitudes of war and may help children to gain some valuable insights into the constant wars that they see on the television around the world, at two stages removed, that is, by time and space. (Although refugee children will know only too well what war means in reality. See book below.)

Hoffman, M., *The Colour of Home*, Frances Lincoln, 2002.
  As a refugee, a little boy from Somalia arrives in Britain, remembering all the horrors of war from which he and his family had fled. But he can't speak any English and he is lonely and isolated and finds everything about his new life drab and grey and sad. He misses the wonderful colours of his home. This moving story describes how he comes to terms with his current situation and discovers new colours. These traumas must be a common experience for all displaced children who are suddenly uprooted because of war or disaster.

Picture books

Aver, M. and Klages, S., *The Blue Boy*, Gollancz, 1992.
  A boy orphaned by war lives with hate, until the man on the moon provides some answers.

Flournoy, V., *The Patchwork Quilt*, Puffin Books, 1995.
  Suitable for 6–7 year olds, the story focuses on love and co-operation in the making of the quilt.

Goffe, T. (Illus), *War and Peace*, Child's Play International, 1992.
  Starting with quarrels in the family, this book goes on to discuss how nations quarrel.

Goffe, T. (Illus), *Charm School*, Child's Play International, 1992.
Cartoon pictures about manners in all sorts of situations. Suitable for 6–7 year olds.

Gowar, M., *A Hard Day's Work*, Andre Deutsch, 1989.
Suitable for 5 year olds. A child causes chaos.

Graham, B., *Crusher is Coming*, Picture Lions, 2000.
Suitable for 5–7 year olds. Crusher turns out to be quite nice.

Hughes, S., *Dogger*, Red Fox, 1996.
A classic story of selfless love, suitable for use with 5–7 year olds, but this story has been used successfully in assemblies, with the whole primary age range.

Hughes, S., *Noisy*, Walker Books Ltd, 2001.
Suitable for the youngest children. Quiet descends at bedtime.

Ikeda, D., *The Cherry Tree*, Oxford University Press, 1991.
The aftermath of war, the flowering tree becomes a symbol of hope.

Isadora, R., *At the Crossroads*, Red Fox, 1993.
South African picture book of children waiting for their fathers to return home from the mines.

Kurtz, J., *Mamo on the Mountain*, Puffin Books, 1997.
A wonderful Ethiopian traditional tale, beautifully illustrated by E. B. Lewis showing sensitively drawn Ethiopians. It is the story of a boy whose parents die and so he sets out to find his sister who works as a cook in a rich man's house. A story of courage and bravery, where good triumphs in the end. Positive black images are reinforced. Some Ethiopian words are introduced. Suitable for 6–10 year olds.

McKee, D., *Tusk, Tusk*, Red Fox, 1993.
Suitable for 7–9 year olds. War between black and white elephants, with a serious peace message.

Mollel, T. M., *The Orphan Boy*, Houghton Mifflin, 1997.
An African mythological tale.

Murphy, J., *Five Minutes Peace*, Walker Books Ltd, 2006.
Mum takes a bath for five minutes peace, but everyone interrupts. Suitable for 5 year olds.

Murphy, J., *Peace At Last*, Macmillan Children's Books, 1995.
Mr Bear cannot find anywhere to sleep that is peaceful. Suitable for 5 year olds.

Oram, H., *Jenna and the Troublemaker*, Anderson Press (new ed.), 2007.
Suitable for 7–11 year olds. A picture book that provokes much good discussion.

Oxenbury, H., *Pig Tale*, Egmont Books, 2004.
The grass looks greener on the other side, but peace is found back at home. 5–7 year olds loved this story, but also it has been used successfully with the whole primary school age range in school assembly.

Ross, T., *I'm Coming to Get You*, Anderson Press, 1984.
Although now one of the 'older' books, it can still be found in libraries. Suitable for six year olds. Comfortingly reassuring as things that frighten turn out to be very small indeed.

Steig, W., *Shrek*, Viking Kestrel Books, 2006.
A popular story about an ugly hero, who marries an ugly princess and finds peace and happiness. All children love this story. It is also available on video/DVD.

Steptoe, J., *Mufaro's Beautiful Daughters. An African Tale*, Puffin Books, 1997.
The beautiful illustrations are inspired by an ancient city in Zimbabwe; the names of the characters are from the Shona language. It is an African version of the Cinderella story, with kindness and generosity to creatures, family, an old woman and a starving boy, that makes one sister fit to marry the King and become his Queen.

Stevenson, J., *The Worst Person in the World*, Kestrel Books, 1996.
An ugly monster befriends the worst person in the world and so becomes a nicer character!

Stones, R., *No More Bullying*, Happy Cat Books Ltd., 2002.
A child who is bullied is rescued by a secondary school pupil helper. Very useful for opening up the whole area of bullying.

Stuve-Bodeen, S., *Babu's Song*, Lee & Low Books, 2003.
Illustrated by Aaron Boyd, it is a lovely Tanzanian tale about a very poor boy, Bernardi, who lives with his mute grandfather, Babu, a toy-maker. Bernardi desperately wants to go to school, but it is too expensive. He also desperately wants a football of his own. He sells his beloved grandfather's music box to buy the ball, but in the end his honesty triumphs and he gives the money back to his grandfather. However, all ends happily. Lovely illustrations of African life.

Tompert, A., *Grandfather Tang's Story* (Ancient Chinese Puzzles), Crown Publications, 1998.
A tale told with 'tangrams'. This is a good story to link with mathematical projects using shapes. The tangrams turn into rabbits, dogs, squirrels, hawks, etc. and finally into geese. The story begins with Fox Fairies who try to out-do each other and then try to help each other. Tangrams are ancient Chinese puzzles. A very useful book for cross-cultural links.

Death Can Bring Peace
Aunty Misery

A powerful story to show children that death is necessary in the natural order of things. The story may help children to discuss death openly and freely and to come to terms with bereavement; perhaps giving children a channel to work through their own grief on the death of a loved one.

The play is adapted by Elizabeth Peirce from an article by Heather Sharpe in the *Times Educational Supplement*, 23 October 1992. The story is believed to be Puerto Rican, although variations have been found in Russia and in Europe.

You will need the following characters

Aunty Misery
A stranger
Four naughty boys
Mr Death
A pear tree
Group of hungry children
Group of old people
Narrator

Aunty Misery
(*Witch-like characterisation.*) My name is Aunty Misery. I hate everyone. I live alone, I am miserable and lonely, miserly and moany. I hate children especially. There are four children in particular, that I dislike more than most. Four stupid boys keep climbing my beloved pear tree and stealing my beautiful pears. They break the branches and rip off leaves; they have even cut the bark of my beautiful tree and carved their stupid names in the trunk. I hate them. I hate, hate, hate them. How I would like to punish them severely.

Narrator
One fine day, a stranger came by Aunty Misery's house and asked her if he could stay the night.

Stranger
Madame, I need shelter for the night and some food. I have travelled a long way and I am very tired and weary. May I stay with you? You will be well paid. I will give you something very special in return for a bed for the night. I will grant you one wish, whatever you want shall be granted.

Aunty Misery
I hate people, but in return for granting my wish: you had better come in and stay the night.

Narrator

So the stranger stayed (*stranger lies down*), but Aunty Misery stayed awake all night, pacing the floor, trying to think how she could use her precious wish. Suddenly, she knew. The very next time the four boys climbed her tree, she would use her wish to trap them in the branches, until they promised to leave her and her tree alone and in peace.

(*Enter four boys.*)

First boy

Come on everyone, quickly, Aunty Misery doesn't appear to be about. Let's steal a juicy pear or two.

Narrator

As the boys clambered into the branches, Aunty Misery came out.

Aunty Misery

Aha, got you, you horrible little creatures. You are now trapped in my tree, forever.

Narrator

Aunty Misery danced a weird little dance around the tree, cackling and spitting with laughter. She pointed with glee as the boys tried to move first their arms and then their legs. It looked as if their hands and legs were stuck in sticky glue. As they tried to lift their limbs, they were pulled back down again as if attached by elastic. (*Boys perform the action.*)

Aunty Misery

Now you have two choices; stay like that forever, or promise never to come here again. Leave me and my tree alone and in peace.

Four boys

(*In unison*) We promise that we will never come near here again. We promise never to harm you or your tree or steal your pears ever again.

First boy

I promise.

Second boy

So do I.

Third boy

Please let us go free, we will never trouble you again.

Fourth boy

Take our word, Aunty Misery, we will never come back.

Aunty Misery

All right then, I will set you free as long as you keep your promise.

Narrator

For a time, all went well, the boys kept their word and never came back. But one fine day, another stranger appeared. His name was Mr Death. He had come to tell Auny Misery that it was time for her to die.

Mr Death
Aunty Misery, I call upon everyone in time, and I have called upon you today, to tell you that it is time for you to die.

Aunty Misery
But I don't want to die, I never want to die, I want to live forever with my beloved pear tree.

Narrator
Aunty Misery thought for a moment. Perhaps the pear tree spell still worked and perhaps she could escape death by trapping Mr Death in her tree as she had trapped the boys long ago. She would set the world free from death forever, if Mr Death was trapped.

Aunty Misery
Oh Mr Death, before I die, could you possibly climb my tree and pick that last remaining pear for me?

Mr Death
Well, as it is your last wish, before you die, yes I will climb up and pick the pear for you.

Narrator
Mr Death climbed up the tree, but to his utter horror and amazement, Mr Death found that he was completely trapped; just like the boys, he could not move his arms or legs.

Aunty Misery
I have conquered death. Ha, ha, no-one will ever die now; nothing will ever die again; everyone and everything will live on for ever and ever.

Narrator
Aunty Misery had indeed trapped death, and nothing and no-one died. But oh dear, soon things began to go very wrong. With nobody dying, the earth soon became overcrowded, then the food ran out and the people began to starve and fight each other for meagre crusts of bread.

Group of hungry children

We are hungry, feed us.
Give me food.
I want food.
That scrap is mine, give it to me.

I'm hungry.
I'm thirsty.
Give me something to eat.
I need food!

(*Children mime the actions.*)

Narrator
And worse was yet to come. As the people got older and older, they got more and more tired and those who were ill cried out to be allowed to die.

Group of old people

Let me die – I am too old to look after myself.
I'm too tired to eat.
I'm too lonely to want to live without my family who died years and years ago.
I'm too ill, I want to die in peace.
Let me die.

(Old people mime the actions.)

Narrator

Mr Death could see what was happening from his vantage point in the tree and so after many years, he decided to make a bargain with Aunty Misery.

Mr Death

If you let me go and restore the natural order of things, with everything dying in its time, I promise that in return, I will let you live on, forever.

Narrator

Aunty Misery agreed. She jumped for joy. Death would be restored in the world. Everything in turn would die, *except* for her. But in the natural order of things, even Aunty Misery's tree died eventually and poor Aunty Misery was compelled to live on and on and on and on, lonely and sad forever and ever and ever.

Prayer

Father God, help us to understand that death is a necessary part of life. Help us to bear the grief and pain when someone we love dearly, dies. Help us to bring your love and comfort to those who are suffering bereavement at this moment. We remember especially (*somebody known to one of the children*) and all his/her family. Bring them your comfort and support in all their sadness. Give them and us, your peace of mind that knows that you are in control, even when things seem to be at their worst. Amen

Hymn

No. 53, 'Peace Perfect Peace' in *Come and Praise*, published by the BBC.

Reflection and poetry

Reflect on the poem below 'Until Gran Died' by Wes Magee in *Morning Break and Other Poems*, published by Cambridge University Press, 1989. Used with very kind permission.

Until Gran died

The minnows I caught
lived for a few days in a jar
then floated side-up on the surface.
We buried them beneath the hedge.
I didn't cry, but felt sad inside.

I thought
I could deal with funerals,
that is until Gran died.

The goldfish I kept in a bowl
passed away with old age.
Mum wrapped him in newspaper
and we buried him next to a rose bush.
I didn't cry, but felt sad inside.

I thought
I could deal with funerals,
that is until Gran died.

My cat lay stiff in a shoe box
after being hit by a car.
Dad dug a hole and we buried her
under the apple tree.
I didn't cry, but felt very sad inside.

I thought
I could deal with funerals,
that is until Gran died.

And when she died
I went to the funeral
with relations dressed in black.
They cried, and so did I.
Salty tears ran down my face.
Oh, how I cried.

Yes, I thought
I could deal with funerals,
that is until Gran died.

She was buried beside an old church
and even the sky wept that day.
Rain fell and fell and fell,
and thunder sobbed far away across the
    town.
I cried and I cried.

I thought
I could deal with funerals,
that is until Gran died.

Wes Magee (with kind permission of the author),
from *Morning Break and Other Poems* by Wes Magee,
Cambridge University Press.

Questions

Has anyone had a pet die? What happened? Did you bury the pet?
Does anyone know a person who has died? What happened?
Why is death necessary?
How can you comfort those who mourn?

Further development

Find out about different religious communities and how they deal with death, funerals
and mourning. For example Yahrzeit (anniversary of a death, Judaism) or Gurpurbs
(death or birth celebrations in the Sikh community).

The Peace Medal

This assembly is based on the true story 'The Cheyenne Way of Peace' by C. Lehn in *Peace Be With You*, published by Faith and Life Press, 1980.

The stories of how the white people treated the North American Indians are horrendous. It is a wonder, in the face of broken treaties and promises, that any of the Indian Chiefs could still teach their people about peace and yet they did.

One very sad, and yet courageous, story relates to the Cheyenne people and the teachings of their Chief, Sweet Medicine. He taught his people that they should try to live in peace, treat strangers as friends and as members of their own tribe.

But in the year 1825, the United States Government asked the Indian people if they could build a road through the Indian territory. The Government promised that they would only travel on the road and not stray on to any other part of the land.

After much discussion, the Cheyenne people agreed, remembering Sweet Medicine's teaching that they should show hospitality to all people. However, the white people did not keep their part of the treaty; they spread all over the Indian territory, killed the buffalo, drank and sold whisky to the Indians, fought and killed each other in angry brawls and brought disease. The Cheyenne people found it harder and harder not to fight back, and harder and harder to keep the peace with the white people.

One Chief called Lean Bear, who followed the teachings of Chief Sweet Medicine, was greatly disturbed by these events. He still wanted to keep the peace with the white people and to live in harmony. So, in 1862, he went to see the President in Washington, to formulate a Peace Treaty. The President agreed with Chief Lean Bear and a Peace Treaty was drawn up and duly signed by the President himself. The President even gave Chief Lean Bear a peace medal as an outward sign of their agreement.

Lean Bear really believed that the President would keep his part of the bargain and so when, soon afterwards, he saw a white army marching towards his camp, he went out to greet them. He wore his peace medal and took with him the signed documents. He told his people not to be afraid as the President himself had promised that they would not come to any harm. But before Chief Lean Bear had a chance to say anything to the soldiers, they shot and killed him.

An angry battle broke out once more. Yet this was not the way of the Cheyenne people. Another Chief, Black Kettle, rode amongst the Cheyenne people and persuaded them to remember the teachings of Chief Sweet Medicine and to keep the peace so that Lean Bear's death would not be in vain. He finally managed to restore order.

This lovely story raises the question of how, even in the face of broken promises and terrible treatment by aggressors, could these forgiving people manage to keep faith with their beliefs?

Perhaps the children could re-enact the story for themselves, making Indian head-dresses and period army caps. The children could find America on a large-scale map and plot the Indian territory with the President in Washington, etc. End the assembly by reading Chief Seattle's lovely poem, which was part of a later speech that he made to the Governor of the Washington territory in 1854, when he was trying to arrange yet another treaty.

How Can One Sell the Air?

We shall consider your offer
to buy our land.
What is it that the White Man wants to
    buy?
my people will ask.

How can one sell the air
or buy the warmth of the earth?
It is difficult for us to imagine.
If we don't own the sweet air
or the bubbling water,
how can you buy it from us?
Each hillside of pines shining in the sun,
each sandy beach and rocky river bank,
every steep valley with bees humming
or mists hanging in dark woods,
has been made sacred by some event
in the memory of our people.

We are part of the earth
and the earth is part of us.
The fragrant flowers are our sisters;
the reindeer, the horse,
the great eagles, are our brothers.
The foamy crests of waves in the river,
the sap of meadow flowers,
the pony's sweat and the man's sweat
are one and the same thing.
So when the Great Chief in Washington
sends word that he wants to buy all these
    things,
we find it hard to understand.

Chief Seattle
(From *Green Poetry*, selected by R. Hull, published by Wayland 1991)

Prayer

Father God, we have seen in this story about the Cheyenne people that even in the face of enormous provocation, the Indian people tried to be peaceful. Help us to live in peace with our neighbours too. Amen

Hymn

No. 85, 'Spirit of Peace' in *Come and Praise 2*, published by the BBC.

Acknowledgements

Albert, D. (*adaptation of a story by the author*): 'Rain Forests: The Tree Huggers', based on *Gaura Devi Saves Trees*. New Society Publishers, 1992.

Arthur, J. (*poem*): 'Peace is Not the Absence of War', in *Voices Speaking Peace*, published by The Unitarian Peace Fellowship, 1990. Used with kind permission.

Bible Society (*'Good News Bible' quotations*): Scriptures and additional materials quoted are from the Good News Bible © 1994, 2004, published by The Bible Societies/HarperCollins Publishers Ltd, UK. Good News © American Bible Society 1966, 1971, 1976, 1992. Used with kind permission.

Birtles, E. (*verse*): 'Let Peace Fill Our Heart', from the longer poem 'Lead Me From Death To Life', in *Voices Speaking Peace*, published by The Unitarian Peace Fellowship, 1990. Used with kind permission.

Burbridge, P.: 'The Parable of the Talents', from *Time to Act* by Paul Burbridge and Murray Watts, published by Hodder & Stoughton, 1979; and (*adaptation of a story by the author*): 'A Judge is Judged' based on 'Judge Not' in *Divine Comedies*, published by Monarch Publications, 1994. Both used with kind permission.

Compston, K. (*poems*): 'Peace is Like Gossamer', from *Leaves From The Tree of Peace*, 1986; and 'New Responsibility' in *Threads of Creation*, 1989; both published by The United Reformed Church. Used with kind permission.

Coombes, D. (*music for hymn*): 'Now the Harvest is All Gathered', in *Come and Praise 2*, published by the BBC. Music by Douglas Coombes, © Lindsay Music (Members of CCLI). Used with kind permission.

CopyCare (*hymn*): 'If I Were a Butterfly', words and music by Brian Howard, © 1974 Mission Hills Music; administered by CopyCare, PO Box 77, Hailsham, East Sussex BN27 3EF, music@copycare.com. Used with kind permission.

De Gay, G. (*poem*): 'Peace Comes', in *Voices Speaking Peace*, published by The Unitarian Peace Fellowship, 1990. Used with kind permission.

Edgecomb, D. (*adaptation of a story by the author*): 'Conservation and Pollution: Cloacina's Story' is based on 'What Now, Cloacina?', in *Spinning Tales, Weaving Hope*, published by New Society Publishers, 1992.

Emery, J. (*two poems*): 'Dance in Front of Tanks' and 'Can Christmas Come for Them?', © John J. Emery. Used with kind permission of his daughter.

Ganeri, A. (*adaptation of a story by the author*): 'Guru Nanak's Needle' is based on 'Duni Chand and Guru Nanak's Needle', from *Sikh Stories*, published by Evans Bros Ltd., 2007. Used with kind permission.

Glick, Hirsch (*words and music of hymn*): 'Zog Nit Keynmol', in *The World's Most Popular Jewish Songs*, published by Tara, 1997.

Henry, O. (*adaptation of a story by the author*): 'A Real Christmas' from *The Third Ingredient*, www.classicreader.com/read.php/bookid.978/sec.1.

Kauter, K. (*adaptation of a story by the author*): 'The Last Snowflake', based on 'The Weight of a Snowflake', in *New Fables, Thus Spoke the Carabou*. www.storybin.com/sponsor/sponsor141.shtmlsponsor141.shtml.

King, Martin Luther (*poem*): 'I Have a Dream', part of a longer speech delivered on 28th August 1963 at The Lincoln Memorial, Washington DC.

Lehn, C. (*adaptation of a story by the author*): 'The Peace Medal', based on 'The Cheyenne Way of Peace', in *Peace Be With You*, published by Faith and Life Press, 1980.

Lipman, D. (*adaptation of a story by the author*): 'Conquering Fear Together' based on 'Chew Your Rock Candy' in *Spinning Tales, Weaving Hope*, published by New Society Publishers, 1992.

Magee, J. (*poem*): 'High Flight', in *The Complete Works of John Magee, The Pilot Poet*, published by This England Books, 1989. Used with kind permission.

Magee, Wes (*poem*): 'Until Gran Died', in *Morning Break and Other Poems*, published by Cambridge University Press, 1989. Used with kind permission.

Masheder, M. (*two games*): 'Getting To Know You' and 'Affirmative Names' from *Let's Play Together* published by Green Print, 1989. Used with kind permission.

Morgan-Hill, Dr. H. (*adaptation of a story by the author*): 'Learning to Love Others: Rainbow Babies' from 'The Rainbow Child', in *Spinning Tales, Weaving Hope*, published by New Society Publishers, 1992.

Moses, B. (*poem*): 'Problems' in *Green Poetry* published by Wayland, 1991.

Nagaraja, Dharmachari (*adaptation of a story by the author*): 'The Dragon at the Wedding'. Used with kind permission.

Nesbitt, E. (*adaptation of a story by the author*): 'A Hindu Story For Jagannath's Rathayatra', is based on the Image of Jagannath in *Listening To Hindus* by Robert Jackson and Eleanor Nesbitt, published by Unwin Hyman Ltd., 1990. Used with kind permission.

Nicholls, J. (*poem*): 'Grudges' in *Storm's Eye* published by Oxford University Press, 1994. Used with kind permission.

Niemoller, Pastor Martin, (*poem*): 'First They Came for the Jews' in *Leaves from the Tree of Peace* published by The United Reformed Church, 1986.

Noyes, A. (*poem*): 'Daddy Fell into the Pond', in *Here We Go Poems* published by Evans Bros Ltd., 1982.

Reeves, J. (*poem*): 'Waiting', in *Complete Poems for Children*, published by Heinemann, 1986.

Rieu, E. V. (*poem*): 'The Hippopotamus's Birthday', in *'The Hippopotamus's Birthday' and Other Poems about Animals and Birds* compiled by L. M. Jennings, published by Hodder & Stoughton Ltd., 1987.

'RSV Bible' Quotations: scripture quoted are from the Revised Standard Version of the Bible copyright © 1946, 1952, and 1971 published by the National Council of the Churches of Christ in the USA. Used by kind permission. All rights reserved.

Schimmel, N. (*adaptation of a story by the author*): 'The Tailor': in *Just Enough To Make A Story. A Source Book For Storytelling*, published by Sister's Choice, 1992. This version was adapted, in turn, from a Yiddish folk tale.

Scholey, A. (*hymn words*): 'Now the Harvest is All Gathered', © Arthur Scholey in *Come and Praise 2*, published by the BBC. Used with kind permission. No part of the words and music may be reproduced in any form, or by any means including photocopying without permission in writing from the publishers, with the exception of the following: (a) holders of a Church Copyright Licence (CCL), who are permitted to reproduce the words according to the terms of their current licence, and (b) holders of a Music Reproduction Licence (MRL), who are permitted to photocopy the music according to the terms of their current licence. For further information about the above licences contact: CCL (Europe), P.O. Box 1339, Eastbourne, East Sussex, BN21 1AD; web site: www.ccl.co.uk e-mail: info@ccli.co.uk phone: 01323 417711.

Seattle, Chief (*poem*): 'How Can One Sell the Air?', in *Green Poetry*, published by Wayland, 1991.

Seremaine, J. (*prayer*): 'Lord You Asked For My Hands', Jo Seremane is Field Liaison Officer, Justice and Reconciliation, South African Council of Churches.

Sharpe, H. (*adaptation of a story by the author*): 'Death Can Bring Peace: Aunty Misery' based on 'Pear Tree of Knowledge' by Heather Sharpe, *Times Educational Supplement*, 23 October, 1992. This story is believed to be Puerto Rican although variations have been found in Russia and in Europe.

Stuart, M. (*poem*): 'The Seed Shop', in *Poems I Remember*, published by Michael Joseph, 1960. Used with kind permission.

Studdert Kennedy, G.A. (*poems*): 'Waste', in *Unutterable Beauty*, published by Hodder and Stoughton, London, 1927.

Topping, F. (*poem*): 'Peace' in *Lord of Life* published by Lutterworth Press, 1982. Reproduced with permission of Curtis Brown Group Ltd, London on behalf of Frank Topping. Copyright © Frank Topping 1982.

Wilde, Oscar (*adaptation of a story by the author*): 'Easter: The Paradise Garden'. Based on a story by Oscar Wilde entitled 'The Selfish Giant', www.classiclit.about.com/library/bl-etexts/owilde/bl-owilde-selgi.htm

The Author would like to thank all the Staff at the East Sussex County Council Schools' Library (Eastbourne Division) for all their help with book research, their welcome, patient answering of all questions and allowing the author access to the latest publications.

Every effort has been made to trace the owners of all copyright material. In one or two cases this has proved impossible. The author will be pleased to correct any omissions in future editions and give full acknowledgements.